T0354693

I Lived Because I Was Loved

I Lived Because I Was Loved

A true story of how *love* and *kindness* helped strangers
facing their own tragedy

TODD AND MARIE IRWIN

I LIVED BECAUSE I WAS LOVED
A TRUE STORY OF HOW LOVE AND KINDNESS HELPED STRANGERS FACING THEIR OWN TRAGEDY

iUniverse books may be ordered through booksellers or by contacting:

iUniverse
1663 Liberty Drive
Bloomington, IN 47403
www.iuniverse.com
844-349-9409

Because of the dynamic nature of the Internet, any web addresses or links contained in this book may have changed since publication and may no longer be valid. The views expressed in this work are solely those of the author and do not necessarily reflect the views of the publisher, and the publisher hereby disclaims any responsibility for them.

Any people depicted in stock imagery provided by Getty Images are models, and such images are being used for illustrative purposes only. Certain stock imagery © Getty Images.

ISBN: 978-1-6632-6545-6 (sc)
ISBN: 978-1-6632-6547-0 (hc)
ISBN: 978-1-6632-6546-3 (e)

Library of Congress Control Number: 2024915787

Print information available on the last page.

iUniverse rev. date: 10/28/2024

PART 1

Our Journeys

As I was waking up from what I thought was a simple exploratory surgery, I asked my wife, Marie, "What did they find?"

She whispered into my ear in a shaky and sweet voice, "It's cancer."

Holy shit, I thought. I immediately answered back, "We will beat it." From my bed in the ICU, I saw two of our three daughters and their husbands with Marie. There was an eerie silence in the room. We all could feel the fear, uncertainty, and sadness. None of us knew the struggle our family would go through to save my life. We sat together wondering what would come next. None of us had experienced cancer with anyone, and we were scared out of our minds.

This is not how we thought our lives would unfold. As every young child learns, to tell someone about a new beginning, one must go back to the start and explain one's journey. We are not going to sugarcoat it. We are going to be honest and raw. We might even make you uncomfortable. But our hope in writing this book and sharing our stories is simple: we all face difficult circumstances, and we want you to see how love and kindness showed up and helped get us through our tough times.

I'm Todd Irwin. Like millions of other people out there, I was diagnosed with and battled cancer. I'll tell you more about my family and story soon. Another person in my story is Glenn Thornton. Glenn is my stem cell donor. But he is so much more than that. He had his own battles while I was living my journey. Glenn is brave, tested, focused, and gracious. We want you to see our stories paralleled in chronological order. Glenn's story will be written by Glenn, and it will parallel my story. You will see also the memories of my wife, Marie, who was my main caregiver and was with me every step of the way. Keep in mind, too, that our family and Glenn did not meet until almost two years into our individual journeys.

Glenn and I did not go on our journeys alone; many other people were important parts of our lives during this time. Following our recollections, we have included some thoughts from our three daughters, members of our family, and some friends who traveled these roads with us. It is important to us for the perspectives of these individuals to be included. This journey affected many people in my life. Each person's contribution is written by him or her and is in his or her voice. Minimal editing was done so you can hear each individual voice. We also did not change contributors' perspectives of incidents, even when they differed from others' accounts. Everyone has his or her own memories, accurate or not, and it's important to see this journey through each person's eyes. None of us are professional writers. Someday you might be the patient, caregiver, child, friend, or donor, and we want you to hear all sides. Our wish is that someone's perspective you read might help you find love and hope if you or a loved one are experiencing turbulent times.

Writing this book has been difficult emotionally, yet it has been therapeutic for all of us. We felt compelled to write it to help others and are glad we did, because through this process Glenn and I have gone from appreciative strangers to true friends. We are each a lifeblood for the other. And love is underneath it all.

Let's start at the beginning.

Todd

July–December 2015

I SEEM TO FIND MYSELF REFERRING TO MY LIFE BEFORE AND AFTER cancer. Even though I spent fifty-six years of my life cancer-free, the two and a half years during which I battled cancer were defining. But there was a day when I wasn't yet a cancer survivor. I lived a wonderful life. I grew up in Columbus, Ohio, one of three boys born to Tom and Gloria Irwin. I had a happy childhood, got in trouble just the right amount, and graduated from The Ohio State University. I married my high school sweetheart, Marie Veatch. After college, I started a good sales career, and we were transferred to Indianapolis. Before we knew it, we had three daughters: Katie, Kelleigh, and Caroline. We built a house on a golf course in Noblesville, Indiana. We were living a contented and busy life. We raised the girls the best we knew how; had a great group of friends; volunteered as coaches for soccer, basketball, and golf; and were involved with our children's schools. Our girls graduated from high school, then college, then graduate schools, and had children of their own. We are very proud parents who never wanted their kids to move out of the house. In fact, I would let all of them move back in with us, but unfortunately, they have not taken me up on my offer.

When I wasn't busy with our kids and work, I was trying to figure out how to perfect my golf swing. I own about every book written on golf and have spent entirely too much money on golf clubs. I was better than average, once a scratch golfer, and had a very skilled short game.

In my thirties I would occasionally have thoughts that

I would someday face a challenge with a difficult illness that I would overcome. As these thoughts popped up more frequently, I felt they came from God, but I would brush them off, thinking my mind was playing games with me. However, I continued to believe that in some strange way it would happen. The message I received was that this would be a real opportunity to show the ones I loved how to deal with difficult challenges. I continued that cavalier attitude until my cancer diagnosis.

I am a happy, optimistic person by nature. I'm loud, funny, at times inappropriate, and quite often the life of the party. I love people: I love talking to them, learning about them, and sharing with them. I'm a pretty emotional guy. I cry easily. I enjoy listening to fun and upbeat music by Kelly Clarkson and Elton John and other artists. I talk trash better than I take it. And despite the fact that I have three daughters, two female dogs, two female guinea pigs, and a wife, I'll never remember that I am not supposed to ask any of our daughters how she got that big pimple on her face.

Marie and I were beginning the prime years of life and getting to a time when our girls weren't sucking us dry of our money after college, graduate school, and weddings. But then that whole "God laughs when we make plans" sentiment became soberingly true when real life reared its ugly head.

During the summer of 2015, I was walking down the fairway at my club, Wolf Run, in Zionsville, Indiana, carrying my golf clubs. I was feeling very tired with an unusual pain in my stomach as my buddy Jim Merton and I approached the fourteenth green. Jim looked at me and said, "You don't look so good. Is everything okay?"

My first thought was *I am just getting old at fifty-six, and I need to lose some weight.* I was the kid who always had to wear husky-size pants! I struggled to finish playing my round, needing some breaks along the way until we finished. After getting home, I took a nap and then felt fine. I played the following day without difficulty. Little did I know this was the beginning of the biggest challenge of my life. My tiredness and infrequent pain continued over the next couple of months, gradually getting worse. I had many tests run, but the doctors could not figure out why I was having so much pain. Early in November, my stomach again just did not feel right, and Marie suggested I go see my general practitioner, Dr. Bill Wunder. He sent me for a CT scan. Nothing unusual was seen on the scan, so because of my stomach discomfort, a colonoscopy and endoscopy were scheduled for the week before Thanksgiving. Nothing was found by the gastroenterologist in those scopes, and I was prescribed some acid reflux medications. I still did not feel like myself, but I continued to work and just get through it.

On the Monday of Thanksgiving week, I took an important business trip to see a customer in Ohio. I worked for a company that installs and sells high-temperature ceramics. On the six-hour drive, I felt as if I were coming down with the flu. On the way back home, I drove through Columbus, Ohio, to pick up my mother-in-law, Marilyn, to bring her to our house for the holidays. When she first saw me, she didn't hesitate to comment that I looked very ill, and I agreed. By Thanksgiving Day, because of the discomfort I could barely eat any of the wonderful food prepared by Marie and Marilyn. And trust me, it takes significant discomfort to turn down food from those two women.

The following Monday morning, I was frustrated with all my lying around doing nothing and decided to take our dog, Charlie, to the pet store to have her nails trimmed. While waiting for Charlie, I ran into the restroom and violently threw up. I had eaten some green Jell-O, just to try to get something in my stomach. I could not get out of the store fast enough. The smell of a pet store is one I never want to relive. All pet stores have lost me as a customer for life. On the drive home, I threw up again all over the car, somehow missing poor Charlie, who was sitting in the front seat. I called Marie, who was at work, and told her something was wrong. Fortunately, I already had a noon doctor's appointment with my general practitioner. Marie came home from work and took me to my appointment. My general practitioner, Dr. Bill Wunder, walked into the room, took one look at me, and sent me to the emergency room so a surgeon could look at me and run some tests. Dr. Wunder also asked the gastroenterologist to see me again. Little did we know that Dr. Wunder had just saved my life.

After a series of tests over a couple of days, including another CT scan, the doctors came up with nothing. The decision was made by the surgeon to schedule exploratory surgery. The doctors explained it could be one of several things, with cancer being the least likely. On December 3, 2015, one hour into the surgery, the surgeon called Marie from the operating room and gave her the worst news possible: he had found a malignant tumor on the outside of my colon where the small and large intestines meet. And the cancer had metastasized to my surrounding lymph nodes. The tumor, many lymph nodes, and fourteen inches of my intestines were removed during an additional four hours of surgery. The tumor had not shown up prominently on the CT scan because of its unusual location.

After a week recovering from surgery in the hospital, we were sent home with names of oncologists recommended by my surgeon. None of them could see me for two to three weeks. We had no idea whom to trust; it was scary. Our good friend Bryan Mills, who is president of Community Health Network in Indiana, including their hospitals, called us when he heard our news. Bryan and his wife, Cathie, lived only a couple of blocks away and came to our house immediately.

Bryan set us up with the best oncologist and the smartest man he knew, Dr. Sumeet Bhatia, for the next morning. How lucky we were to receive this blessing from God. Bryan could not believe other oncologists would not be able to see me for two to three more weeks. If I had waited to see one of those oncologists, I would have died.

It's important to note that I would not have survived the illnesses I am about to describe without the total dedication of my wife, Marie, as a caregiver. I first met her when we were in the third grade. We were eight years old. She moved from Ashland, Kentucky, to Columbus, Ohio, just before school started in 1967. This pretty, shy blonde girl had to stand up in front of our class and introduce herself. I will never forget her introduction, "Hi, y'all. My name is Jean Marie," she said with her southern twang. The entire class laughed, as most had never heard a southern accent. She sat down and buried her head in her arms in embarrassment.

I'm not exactly sure when I first started paying attention to Marie. I was a school safety crossing guard in sixth grade, and I remember Marie walking by my patrol post, hiding her face behind her books because of her shyness—or maybe because I was really ugly! I do remember holding her hand in the gym in sixth grade when the lights turned off for a movie, and that's when I discovered that her hands were incredibly soft. Her hands are still just as soft today. I bought her a going-steady ring at Hart's, a general department store in Columbus. She wore it for two weeks before she had a girlfriend ask me to close my eyes as the ring was placed in my hand. That was my first broken heart. In eighth grade, we were in the same choir class, where she sat behind me, and I would always sneak looks at her because she was so beautiful.

We finally got back together during our junior year of high school. Marie always laughed at what I considered to be romantic—for example, my call to her to ask her to the

5

homecoming dance. Our dialogue went as follows: "Hi, Marie, this is Todd. Do you want to go to the homecoming dance with me?"

"Yes," Marie replied.

"Okay, bye," I said, and I hung up the phone.

Obviously, I wasn't much of a conversationalist! We did attend the dance together and continued to date afterward.

I worked at the local IGA grocery as a bagger and stock boy in Columbus. Marie and I lived in the same neighborhood, and one day as she stood in line at the store, I had a clear vision that I was going to marry this girl. We were inseparable from high school through college at The Ohio State University and have now been married for thirty-eight years. Who would have guessed that the girl I fell in puppy love with would save my life? Marie's wisdom, strength, and determination are unmatched. And, boy, am I glad she chose me to love.

Marie

December 2015

NUMB. I WAS IN A FROZEN, NUMB HAZE. I COULD BARELY BREATHE. I was standing at the volunteer station in the surgery waiting room, holding a receiver, listening to my husband's surgeon tell me he had cancer. Probably lymphoma. And it was bad. Surgery would take another three to four hours. *What? No, no, no. This was exploratory surgery. The last thing they thought it would be was cancer. A tumor? It had spread into his lymph nodes? Colon resection?* My mind was spinning. *Our girls. How do I tell our three daughters?* I had no answers to their questions. I knew nothing about cancer. Nothing about treatment. Nothing about oncologists. Nothing about Todd's chances of survival. I stared into space. My mouth was so dry. I was nauseated. *The boy I met when I was eight years old, married when I was twenty two—he might not be here soon.* They need a padded soundproof room in hospitals—a place to go scream and cry and pound out your fear and anger. This wasn't fair. What in the world was God thinking?

For a couple of months leading up to this horrible day, Todd was not himself. At first we thought it was just a virus and he was run down. Todd likes to go through his days at breakneck speed. There is never enough daylight for him. More than once he has mowed the yard in the dark with the mower headlights on! After many doctors, tests, procedures, and medications, with only worsening symptoms, Todd's general practitioner took one look at him on November 30, 2015, and pulled out his phone to call the surgeon. We went straight to the hospital, and Todd was admitted. Three days

7

later, we received the worst news of our lives. I remember the word "gobsmacked" going through my mind. I'm a planner and always prepared. We could not have been less prepared for cancer. Now what would happen?

Todd and I raised our girls to be empathetic, resilient, flexible, and supportive. When life got tough, it was time to do what we could about it and then move forward. I didn't look back, just as my dad taught me. We have always been each other's biggest supporters and best friends. We have also always shown our daughters a lot of affection, but we were pretty strict. (I was the mom that actually called other parents to be sure that adult supervision would be at a party.) We expected them to earn our trust through their choices and actions. Every time they left the house, I said, "I love you. Make good decisions." I also said it to their friends, and if I forgot, they asked me to say it. Todd and I are very proud that when we received his diagnosis, our girls helped give our family strength to move forward. But watching them all have to grow up completely in about an hour was also heartbreaking.

After surgery, Todd was admitted to the ICU. The girls and our sons-in-law took over the ICU waiting room. We took turns going to sit with Todd. He had a fourteen-inch bowel resection to remove the tumor attached to his small and large intestines, and his surgeon worked so hard to remove as many of the cancerous lymph nodes as he could. I think he was as devastated as we were at what he found. I was advised not to tell Todd about the cancer at first. I knew that decision was mine though. As I watched Todd sleep, so many memories flew through my mind: high school parties that we went to after football games, walking to class together in college, his marriage proposal while sitting on a bright yellow furry sofa at his parents' house (there is nothing like seventies décor!), becoming parents, watching him coach our daughters in various sports, walking two of our daughters down the aisle at their weddings, seeing him be an awesome grandfather to his first two grandchildren. I knew I couldn't lie to him. And I did not want our kids to see me lie to him. So when he woke up, his first question was "Do I have cancer?"

I replied, "Yes ... but we are going to do whatever it takes to beat it," and that became our family goal—whatever we had to do.

Just as Todd had a premonition about something happening, I also had one. I remember this moment as if it happened today. I was sitting in my chair in the family room of the house where we raised our girls. I remember thinking how much I loved our normal, quiet, unassuming life. And then I felt a cold chill, and I knew something was going to happen to someone close to me. I felt it in my gut. I knew my normal was going to change. It was a terrifying moment. I thought about it for a few weeks afterward with a "When is it going to happen?" feeling. And it did not hit me when Todd was hospitalized at first. It hit me when I put the phone receiver to my ear in the hospital waiting room and listened to the doctor say, "Todd has cancer." This was it. My heart literally ached.

Todd

December 2015

MY INITIAL DIAGNOSIS WAS A LYMPHOMA THAT WOULD REQUIRE ONE day of chemotherapy every three weeks at the cancer center. However, Dr. Bhatia had my pathology report rerun by his lab, and unfortunately there was a new diagnosis of Burkitt's lymphoma. Burkitt's is a rare B-cell non-Hodgkin lymphoma that typically occurs in children and young adults. There is no such thing as a good cancer, but on the scale of sucky cancers to really sucky cancers, this was really sucky. And I was in stage IV. I knew stage IV wasn't good, but the doctor felt I had a chance, and that's all I needed to hear. Dr. Bhatia first pointed out that getting cancer was not any fault of the patient and that the cancer could have been in my body for a very long time and been triggered by something. But none of that mattered; we just needed to focus on getting rid of it. He explained that this cancer was very aggressive but if we treated it with chemo aggressively, we could conquer it. Dr Bhatia made me feel everything would be okay. I would soon learn exactly what he meant by "aggressive" treatment.

I was back home recovering from surgery in mid-December, and learned my chemotherapy would start in four weeks. With the new diagnosis of Burkitt's, I would have five to six days of continuous chemo as an inpatient at the hospital—pure poison that I had to have run through my body to have any chance of survival. My white cell count would go down to zero with each round of chemo. Your white cells help your body fight off infection and disease, so this meant I had zero immunity to any germs. I would stay at the hospital until my white cell count was high enough to provide me some immunity. I would have one week of inpatient chemo every three weeks for six rounds. Was I scared? Yes. Was I confused? Yes. Did I realize what I would go through in the months to come? Clueless. Everything was going so fast. There wasn't time to think or make decisions. All I knew was that I had to stay in the present moment. I could not dwell on the past or worry about the future. I needed to direct all my strength to the present moment and trust my medical team.

So I had four weeks to recover from major bowel resection surgery. Or so I thought. On a Sunday afternoon right before Christmas, I felt terrible. My colon resection surgery had been less than two weeks prior. A piercing pain in my stomach sent me to my bed. I was curled up trying to rest when Marie came in and asked me what was wrong. I told her I thought I needed to go to the hospital. The pain I was having was scary; I'd never felt pain like that before. She took me straight to Community Hospital North ER, in Indianapolis. We didn't know what was going on.

As I lay in the ER, my entire family gathered as we waited for some information. I remember questions bouncing around from everyone to Dr. Bhatia. I knew they were talking about me, but I was in so much pain I couldn't even ask any questions. All of these people standing around me had more control over me than I had over myself. The conclusion was that we had to trust Dr. Bhatia's recommendation to begin chemotherapy immediately. I am glad we put that trust in him. My chemotherapy was starting two weeks earlier than any doctor advised. I was petrified. The big question was, Would the chemo drugs blow out my colon resection?

My first treatment started with a drug called rituximab. One hour into the treatment, I felt the worst pain I had ever felt in my life. The nurse said I was just anxious, and I told her, "Bullshit!" I remember screaming for our youngest daughter,

Caroline, to go get help. Caroline remembers this as a *Grey's Anatomy* moment with no McDreamy on the other end! I was shaking, begging, panicking, and demanding they do x-rays to determine whether they were damaging my intestines where the surgery was performed. I received painkillers, and x-rays confirmed no damage. Dr. Bhatia explained that the pain I felt was caused by rituximab killing the cancer. It was freaky to have this drug eating away at the cancer monster in my body. My imagination saw all these tiny blobs of cancer being burned away.

We learned which chemo drugs I would be given the day after I was admitted to the hospital. One three-week period was considered one round. The first week, I was given various chemo medications around the clock for six to seven days. When my white count was high enough, I would be discharged home. The second week, we visited the cancer center every other day for more chemo, fluids, blood, or platelet transfusions. Week three was for recovery and more fluids, blood transfusions, platelets—whatever was required by frequent blood tests at the cancer clinic. This would be repeated for six rounds.

As part of my first four chemo treatments, I would also receive chemo to stop the cancer from spreading to my brain. This was important, because if the cancer got to my brain, I was a dead duck. This involved being placed on a tilted table where they injected chemo into my spinal fluid. The procedure was extremely stressful. I knew I had to have the treatment, but having chemo for my brain was daunting to say the least. The doctor who administered my brain chemo was Dr. Perry Wethington, and he calmed me by talking about golf. When I was able to play golf after recovery, we were unknowingly paired in a group together at our golf course. Several holes into the round, we discovered our connection. Perry couldn't believe it and was very happy that I had survived. Little did I know that was the beginning of a friendship, as we now enjoy playing golf together frequently. After each treatment, I had to lie flat with little movement for eight hours. You can use your own imagination as to how I peed!

During my inpatient chemo weeks, I would often have two or three bags of chemo going at the same time. My regimen was full of very strong drugs with many side effects. I was monitored closely by my medical team for any signs that any of the drugs were harming my organs or health in detrimental ways. One drug, doxorubicin, is nicknamed "Red Devil" for its red color and difficult side effects. It can cause heart damage. There is a lifetime limit on the amount of doxorubicin a person can receive. Knowing this made watching these drugs going into my body very scary, but without them I would not survive. The prices for some bags of chemo were astronomical. Many of the drugs were priced in the many thousands of dollars. The hospital didn't offer any high-volume pricing discounts either! After a week of treatment, I was able to go home. The side effects typically began ten days after the beginning of the first treatment and lasted seven to ten days. My hair began falling out within a couple of weeks of my first chemo round. While I didn't have much hair on my head at age fifty-six, I had plenty on the rest of my body. Our family hairstylist, Debbie, graciously came and shaved me to just get it over with. While chemo often causes hair loss, Marie noticed quickly that it did not cause my ear or nose hair to stop growing!

Trips back and forth to the cancer clinic were very difficult in weeks two and three of each round. The painful side effects are cumulative, meaning the effects are worse during each successive round. I became weaker and weaker the further I got into my treatments. Just sitting in the car for the trip to the cancer center was painful. My bones ached, and I had very low energy levels. I often had chemo brain fog caused by the very toxic drugs that had been pumped into my body. It felt as though I couldn't think for myself, and I always had a bad headache that made me feel as if I were in an alternate reality.

After each chemo round, I would receive injections in my stomach to help improve my blood counts. Dr. Bhatia referred to weeks one and two as "being in jail" and week three as "being out of jail"; it's a good description. As I sat in the cancer center waiting room with whoever had brought me during weeks two and three, it was depressing to observe all the patients wearing sweatpants, sitting in wheelchairs with bald heads and wigs, all looking exhausted. And I was one of them! Eventually we would talk about our treatments. As we compared our chemo treatments, I came to realize how sick I really was. I was in the minority, as I met no other patients who were receiving anything close to the amount of chemo I was getting. Wow, I was very sick!

Marie and I would learn that being discharged from the hospital and going home can feel very strange. My body was messed up, and I had been sleeping in an uncomfortable bed where a nurse woke me every two hours for vitals and meds. When I was discharged, I went outside to fresh air, sunshine, and trees, and back home where I belonged. What a contrast! Marie and I usually cried at the beginning of each trip home.

Marie

December 2015–January 2016

WHEN TODD WAS DIAGNOSED WITH THE BURKITT'S, I DID NOT DO any research on it. I know that sounds kind of crazy, but after we were told the news, I was in a fragile mental state. Todd, Katie, Kelleigh, and I had gone to the cancer center for our chemo teach class. We were going to learn what we could expect with the chemo treatments that would occur once every three weeks on an outpatient schedule. After a very long wait, we were taken to a patient room and told it would be a bit before we would see Dr. Bhatia. I instantly knew something was wrong, and my anxiety went through the roof. As I paced in the tiny room, the girls tried to calm my fears, but I knew this was not going to go well. We learned that day that Todd did not have the "easy" lymphoma (if there is such a thing) that would require treatment on an outpatient basis every three weeks. We learned that his treatment would still be every three weeks but would entail inpatient hospitalizations of a week or more for every treatment, of which there would be six treatments. As my brain and heart tried to process this information, I had to make what I called survival decisions. I had to protect some portion of my sanity, and in order to do that I knew I could not look at survival rates, treatment options, chemo side effects, and such. So in that moment I chose to listen to and trust Dr. Bhatia and his team, which also included MD Anderson doctors. They had the best research and experience with Burkitt's. They were the experts. I knew I had to focus on Todd and help him heal from his surgery and gain strength, and I knew I had to show a very brave

15

face to the kids and Todd. I knew I had to keep working full-time to keep our insurance. So I surrendered to the medical professionals to tell me what I needed to know and to God to somehow push me through what was going to be a major life-and-death battle for my husband. We never did receive our chemo teach session. But we learned quickly and figured things out as we went along.

On Sunday, December 20, 2015—two weeks and four days after Todd's major bowel resection surgery—I went upstairs to check on him. While he seemed to be recovering from the surgery, it felt as if he had been going a little backward the past couple of days. When I got upstairs, I found him pale and doubled over in pain. He begged me to take him to the ER. I had no idea what was wrong, so I loaded him into the car; and as we left the house, I called Cathie Mills, Bryan's wife, to see if she could get a message to Bryan, and possibly Dr. Bhatia, that something was very wrong with Todd and we were headed to Community Hospital North ER. As soon as the kids heard, they headed to the ER as well. The ER started the usual battery of tests: blood work, CT scan, and so on. By the time Dr. Bhatia arrived, all of us were crammed into that little ER room, and everyone was extremely concerned about what was happening. I think there were nine of us there: Todd, myself, Katie, Eric (Katie's husband), Eric's brother, Kelleigh, Drew (Kelleigh's husband), Bryan Mills, and Dr. Bhatia. I'm sure the ER staff were not too happy with us—but with the hospital CEO there, I'm sure they knew not to say anything! Dr. Bhatia told us Todd's Burkitt's lymphoma had returned with a vengeance.

Dr. Bhatia told us that chemo needed to start as soon as possible. Todd was two weeks and four days out from his bowel resection surgery. We had been advised that chemo couldn't start until four to six weeks after surgery for fear of his intestines blowing out. So now we were faced with a horrifying decision. But we really didn't have a decision to make. Waiting several more days, much less two more weeks, could mean certain death for Todd. Burkitt's lymphoma is known as the fastest-growing human tumor. (I did eventually google it after he reached remission. I'm still glad I didn't google it any sooner!) Blessedly Todd and I had spent the entire week prior to the ER visit completing all the tests needed to begin chemotherapy, and his first port had been implanted in his chest. Throughout his treatment, he would have three different types of ports: a Port-a-Cath, a PICC line, and a Hickman line. These ports are used to carry any chemotherapy drugs, medications, or fluids into the body. I'm sure Dr. Bhatia scheduled these tests and port surgery when he did because he knew this could happen.

Chemo began the evening of December 21, 2015. Todd's first three chemotherapy rounds were the hyper-CVAD with rituximab regimen. Caroline arrived from Chicago to Todd's room about the time the rituximab was started. It was late in the evening, about 9:00 p.m. Rituximab is an antibody therapy that helps the body attack and kill cancer cells. Todd's lymphoma had spread into his stomach area, and the extreme pain he experienced was the drug doing exactly what it was supposed to do—killing cancer cells! We did not know this at the time and learned it only the next day. Todd's pain began escalating about the time Caroline arrived. I had been at the hospital since we had gone to the ER the day before. I'm sure I looked a mess; I had on the same clothes and hadn't showered or slept. But I wasn't going to leave just as they began the chemo. And I'm glad I didn't. Todd was starting to get very uncomfortable and was beginning to moan. I called the nurse, who told him he was just experiencing anxiety. Huh? I had never heard anyone moan with anxiety. I told the nurse I didn't think that's what it was. After all, I knew Todd best and would know his signs of stress and worry. But she left, and

Caroline and I tried to calm Todd down. But it just continued to escalate. I finally sent Caroline to the nurses' station to get help. After a second trip to the nurses' station by Caroline, and after other staff came in to check on Todd, it was finally determined that something else was going on, and Todd was given pain meds. No relief. Todd was begging the nurses to stop the chemo. The hospitalist doctor came in, and after he talked to Dr. Bhatia, they gave Todd a lot more pain meds and ordered an x-ray to check his intestines. Now, this entire time Todd was writhing in pain and yelping "Oh, oh, oh!" constantly. We really thought he might die. It was very surreal, but I knew I had to stay calm and in the moment. I wanted to run and scream, "For God's sake, someone help my husband!"

A hospital escort arrived to take Todd down to have the x-ray. As they started down the hall, Todd was begging the poor escort to turn off the treatment. I finally just told Todd it had been stopped so the poor young man taking him wouldn't have to listen to Todd plead! Fortunately the x-ray showed no damage. Eventually, after several different pain medications were given to Todd, they were able to control the pain. Either that or the rituximab had completed its job. That rituximab was a frightening and horrible, yet necessary, step to what I believe brought Todd to remission.

We had tried to wait and start Todd's chemo after Christmas. Todd was on day four of chemo on Christmas Day. I went to the hospital in the morning, and the kids came for the afternoon. Some of Kelleigh's coworkers had brought some Christmas decorations that we put up. While we tried to enjoy the time together, it was a somber day. I have a picture of the patient information dry erase board from Todd's room for December 25, 2015. Rereading the information on the board brings back sadness and fearful feelings. The board also had one of the many nicknames we gave to Dr. Bhatia on it; "Dr. Analogy." This holiday was the first of many we would celebrate in the hospital, along with anniversaries and birthdays. Using the word "celebrate" is probably an overstatement.

After round one of chemo, I was so happy when he was discharged. The drive home was quiet since the effects of chemo had started and Todd did not feel that great. The happy feeling stopped about the time I helped Todd into bed at home and realized it was just me and him. I had no backup: no nurses, no doctors, no nurse assistants, no meals from the hospital meal service, no one to ask for advice. I of course had medical staff I could call at any time, but I had to make the decision as to when I should call them. I was very overwhelmed, but I knew I had the ability to do what was needed to take care of Todd.

Let's just say subsequent discharges did not hold the same joy as the first one. At Todd's second discharge, his nurse for the day, Erin, was so kind. I think she saw that I had a bit of apprehension about taking Todd home. She asked me how I was feeling, and I was very honest and told her I was scared. She sat me down and encouraged me, telling me I could call the medical renal oncology (MRO) floor at the hospital anytime, day or night, for help, and she felt confident I could handle everything. I really appreciated that she even recognized how afraid I felt. Again, nurses rock!

Todd

January–March 2016

DURING THESE CHEMO ROUNDS, THE NUMBER OF PILLS I TOOK A day was insane: fifteen or so for breakfast and another twenty or so throughout the rest of the day. I do not want to complain but want people to know what to expect. Side effects included fatigue, headaches, endless diarrhea, bone pain, chemo brain, neuropathy, syncope, hair loss, thrush, nausea, muscle weakness, weight loss, and muscle fatigue. I had a body I was not familiar with. The fatigue was like having the flu; it would literally suck the energy out of me. The diarrhea was sometimes occurring so frequently that it would wear out the old rectum, requiring special creams after each bowel movement. It gave a whole new meaning to having what I call "red ass"! I felt like one of those monkeys with the red butts in *National Geographic*!

The bone pain was a chilling effect running through my bones. The steroids I had to take caused my muscles and bones to ache. It felt as if my bones might shatter from the cold that ran through them. And the chemo was damaging my nerves, causing neuropathy, which feels like needles being stuck into the skin of my hands and calves and feet. This started in my feet and hands and eventually moved to the rest of my body as chemotherapy continued. There were no remedies to relieve this pain. We tried creams and medications, but the pain was always there. While the neuropathy still affects me today, it has improved, but it may never completely go away. Medication has helped, but nothing has provided complete relief.

The most bizarre side effect of my chemotherapy was the

random passing out, called syncope. Syncope is the loss of consciousness when your blood pressure plummets. And my blood pressure had started dropping every time I stood. I was at home by myself after the first round of chemo. After I woke up, I went downstairs; and the next thing I knew, I was regaining consciousness on the kitchen floor in a pool of sweat. My muscles in my body were spasming, I was disoriented, and I had to go to the bathroom. I managed to call Marie at work. I was not thinking straight, because I should have called 911. I managed to crawl to the bathroom—which was stupid—and peed. My body continued to spasm, and I could not move to get in the right position to relieve the muscles. Marie called Eric, our son-in-law, and then 911. Eric was the first to arrive, as he was the closest to our house at his job as an assistant principal at a school about five miles away. Eric arrived, and he gave me a big hug and held on to me to give me some relief until the ambulance arrived. It was certainly the most intimate moment I'd ever had with my son-in-law! Marie wasn't too far behind, and she found Eric—who is six foot three—and me huddled together on our bathroom floor. It's a half bath and very small, so it must have looked a little crazy to her!

The ambulance arrived, and the EMTs got my vitals under control and decided I needed to be transported to the Community Hospital North ER. En route, we learned that the hospital emergency room was full, so the ambulance diverted to take me to another hospital. I handed my phone to the EMT and told him to call Dr. Bhatia. He looked at me strangely, and about that time my phone rang, and it was Dr. Bhatia. My wife had already called him—surprise, surprise.

Dr. Bhatia is extremely intelligent, highly educated, and well respected in his field of oncology. He takes medical courses for fun. He is also kind, patient, and has an impressive bedside manner. When mild-mannered Dr. Bhatia told the EMT to bring me to the cancer center and the EMT commented that they were only authorized to take patients to hospital emergency rooms, Dr. Bhatia calmly told the EMT, "I am authorizing you."

The EMT said, "Yes sir," and took me to Community MD Anderson Cancer Center North. This is how Dr. Bhatia earned his nickname "Dr. Badass." At first he was a bit indifferent to his new nickname, but it grew on him, and I think he even grew to really like it. We pulled up to the cancer center, and if you had been there, you would have thought I was the president, as numerous nurses, nurse practitioners, Dr. Bhatia, Marie, and Eric were waiting for me. Caroline wished she had been there for that *Grey's Anatomy* moment. Passing out like this was not a common side effect, so there was great concern.

After I had spent a couple of days in the hospital, they were still unable to figure out why I was passing out. With all the variables going on with my treatments, it was no wonder they never figured out the issue. This random passing out went on for nine months or so, resulting in me rarely being left alone, which was a huge burden on my friends and family. We tried to manage the syncope with all the recommended solutions, but we never got it under control.

After round two of chemo, Mike Murray, a great friend whom I have known since fifth grade, came from Minneapolis to take care of me so Marie could continue working. We went to school with each other from middle school all the way through college. Marie and I double-dated with Mike and his wife, Dayna, through high school and college. One night during the week Mike was helping out, I got up at about 2:00 a.m. to go to the bathroom. The next thing I knew, two people were slapping me in the face. I said, "Stop slapping me in the face." Mike and Marie were sort of laughing, telling me I had passed out. I had to learn the hard way to take my time when getting up. I would first sit up and not move for about a minute, then try to stand up. I typically would get dizzy and need to sit down a couple of times before I could stand. Later that day, Mike and Marie put together a bedside toilet for me. This was a lot different than the double dates we went on in high school. I thought, *Really! Am I that pathetic?* It was another humbling experience. The bedside toilet became a part of our bedroom furniture for a long time.

● ● ●

Following is a side note from Marie:

The night Todd passed out, I saw him start to fall as he headed to the bathroom, and I leaped out of bed and managed to somewhat gently lower him to the floor. Then I ran to where Mike was sleeping and yelled for help. He jumped up, and we both ran back to Todd, where we started trying to bring him back to consciousness. We both did start laughing when Todd told Mike to stop slapping him. And we really started laughing when we realized that I was bent over and my nightgown was gaping open and Mike was sprawled in his undies as we sat on either side of Todd. I'm pretty sure we never envisioned this scenario when we were double dating as sixteen-year-olds!

● ● ●

We were getting to know the routine of the side effects of a round of chemo better. We could tell when I needed fluids, a blood transfusion, or platelets before the blood work came back, based on how I was feeling. My incredible brother-in-law, Peter, volunteered to come up from Lexington to take care of me for two weeks. Peter is a very loving and likeable person, and a great cook. We always have good conversations about sports, politics, and other topics. I will never forget when

Peter said that taking care of me helped him more than me. What a wonderful person!

The fourth chemo round would be a critical round, as they would run a scan after it to determine whether my cancer was in remission. The cumulative effect of the chemo was really starting to weaken me. I lost about one hundred pounds in all throughout my treatments. Yes, I was a fat-ass when things started, but my body was starting to look emaciated, with nonexistent muscles, and my limbs sticklike. Marie took a couple of pictures of me at this point. I've never looked at those pictures. Marie says they are hard for her to look at now.

Each treatment continued to beat me up more and more. It was like a boxing match, and I was in the fourth round. I was not winning the match. After each round, they took me to the corner, gave me blood transfusions, plasma transfusions, fluids, and shots to boost my white blood cell counts. They'd get my blood counts back up enough just to send me back into the ring for another chemo round! Then I would get the shit kicked out of me even worse than the round before. The worst side effect is what it does to your mind. It was like having a permanent concussion. I couldn't think too clearly, but I just got out there and did the best I could.

On March 11, I had a PET scan. Three days later, we received great news. The results of the scan showed I was in complete remission! That was miracle number one. Yet, what did remission really mean? What if there was the tiniest bit of cancer left inside me? Did I want a life that was a cancer roller coaster with no quality of life? I decided remission meant I was okay for now. It meant I was winning. And based on what we had been through, it was a big milestone and cause for celebration.

Marie

January 2016

TODD ENDED UP BACK IN THE HOSPITAL FOR A FEW DAYS AFTER MANY of his chemo rounds. He would pass out and fall or spike a fever, and back he went. He received his first blood transfusion during one of these inpatient visits and was to be discharged as soon as it was over. He experienced an allergic reaction to the infusion, which delayed us leaving the hospital until early evening. Of course we needed to pick up new medications at the pharmacy on the way home. As we drove toward our pharmacy, I saw flashing lights everywhere; and as we got closer, I saw yellow caution tape blocking the entrances. Todd just wanted to get home to his own bed and was already not happy that we had to stop for meds. He could not be left alone, so I had no choice but to stop. And now I couldn't even get into the store! Apparently there had been an attempted robbery at the store. And I have to tell you, I was livid with the person who decided a robbery would be a good idea when I was extremely tired, cranky, and had a sick husband who needed medications. And then it all became so funny to me. Stress laughing is so good for you! Perspective is everything, especially for someone under stress. We drove home laughing—something we hadn't done enough of lately—and it helped lighten the load we both were feeling. The medication would just have to wait until tomorrow.

Caregiving is hard. The most difficult part for me was accepting that I needed help. The next most difficult thing was asking for that help. But we have amazing friends and family who did not accept my answer when I turned them down. Meals began appearing in our refrigerator or were on the doorstep when I arrived home. Friends and family volunteered to help take care of Todd. After round two of chemo, it became apparent that Todd needed 24-7 care. At first our daughters and sons-in-law took turns taking care of Todd. We thought it would be temporary, but Todd's condition after each treatment continued to spiral downward. He was weaker, in more pain, eating less and less, and in need of help doing just about everything. And then our friends and family began volunteering to help take care of him for a week at a time so I could continue working, which was necessary to keep our medical insurance and give the kids some relief. This wasn't just taking care of a person that didn't feel good. Todd was passing out on a regular basis, had to be helped to shower, needed to be helped up and down steps, was using a bedside toilet, was taking more than thirty medications daily, and had to be dressed and taken to the cancer center every day or two. These wonderful people *volunteered*! I remember a weekend when we didn't have anyone coming to help for the following week, which meant I would have to take more of my dwindling Family and Medical Leave Act (FMLA) days. I tried very hard to reserve these days for times when I knew Todd would need my support or need me to advocate for him. It was Sunday afternoon, and Todd's phone rang. A good friend from our childhood, Jimmy Gulick, called and said, "Hey, I was thinking about coming over this week if you could use the help." And when a second childhood friend, Rocco Morando, found out Jim was coming, he wanted to come as well. God answered my very stress-filled, not-worded-in-the-nicest-way prayers. They were more requests than prayers, but God understood and answered. We are so blessed.

Knowing what to do for anyone in crisis is hard. Ask yourself what you would appreciate if you were experiencing a crisis. Whatever that is will probably be helpful to someone else. Any act of kindness that is done with love is a perfect way to help someone. First and foremost, please pray. We felt those prayers on our darkest days and all the days in between. Feeling that God had our backs gave us some greatly needed peace. Please get swabbed through Be the Match or DKMS, the marrow donor registries. Simply search "Be the Match," or "DKMS" to join the registry. You will be mailed a swab kit to complete. The kit and donating costs nothing but your time, and you could save someone's life! One of our daughters was recently found to be a match for someone. Ultimately she wasn't needed, but she was ready and willing to donate.

Other things that helped us included meals that could be easily heated and transported. Chemo patients have dietary restrictions during certain times of treatment, especially when they are neutropenic, which causes them to be highly susceptible to infection because of low blood counts. Everyone graciously followed those guidelines. At one point, we had a battle of chicken and noodle recipes! It was the exact comfort food we needed. Each meal felt like a warm hug to us. For weeks after Todd was diagnosed, everything tasted like cardboard to me. I didn't have time to go to the grocery, much less cook. We didn't need much; the simpler, the better. Those meals filled our stomachs and our souls. Gift cards to the grocery, big-box stores, and restaurants, as well as gas cards, were also helpful. I filled up my gas tank every other day. I was petrified that I would be low on gas and Todd would need to be taken to the ER!

Cards and notes from all over the country reminded us that so many people cared and were thinking of us. We have a large bin full of cards and letters he received. When Todd could have visitors (though the thought of germs made this so difficult for me), brief visits were helpful for his recovery. We lost all normalcy during this battle. Having friends just come over and talk about normal things was a relief to the medical treatment that our life revolved around. The days that Todd had visitors at the hospital while I was at work helped my guilt at not being able to always be there. Sweet friends brought an amazing memory foam mattress pad that was a godsend for his extremely uncomfortable hospital bed. One of our friends would hang a bag of the best ginger cookies I have ever tasted on our door, and they were a wonderful surprise when I would get home at night. Even seeing that someone had pulled my trash can up to my garage door for me on trash day or that the kind neighbor boy had cut our grass was so helpful.

I did draw the line at someone else doing my personal laundry. No one else was going to fold my underwear. (And yes, I fold my underwear!)

As a caregiver, time for myself didn't exist. The chronic stress left me very fatigued. I adopted some weird routines and habits to help me get to places faster and gain as much time as possible for sleep. I cut back my daily routines as much as possible. I wore the same black pants to work as many days as I dared and threw on the same easy-to-wash tops over and over. (Big thanks to my coworkers for never commenting on this!) I wore the same earrings every day for almost two years. For a year and a half, I kept a completely packed suitcase in the car so I would always be ready to stay with Todd if needed. I never let my gas tank dip below half a tank. I made sure I prayed every night before I went to sleep. I had let my faith slip after my dad died suddenly when I was a young mother. Now, I am not saying I was great at praying and that I wasn't quite displeased with God! I yelled and screamed and cried to him on most days while driving home from the hospital. My conversations with him were not always very polite, and I pleaded a lot. A good friend, Cathie Mills, told me something that changed my faith. I felt I was asking for too much from God when I prayed. She immediately shook her head no and said, "You can never ask for too much; always *pray boldly!*"

28

I was confused. It was okay to ask for specific things. And with fervor! And so I began praying boldly, several times a day. I stopped worrying about asking for too much. I asked God for complete healing, strength to get through the next hour, the chance to go on a date with my husband again, help to stay awake at work, stamina for my children, and that my grandchildren would get to play with Pops (Todd) again. Once Cathie encouraged me, I couldn't be stopped!

Another small blessing in our journey was that I never once got sick. If I had, I wouldn't have been able to see Todd. I made sure I kept up my normal annual appointments with doctors, squeezing them in where I could. I do remember one day when I woke up with a sore throat. I told my body that was not happening. I needed to be at the hospital after work. The sore throat disappeared during the day, and that was that!

It was heartbreaking to see Todd receive enormous amounts of very strong chemo and become weaker each month. The side effects of each round of chemo were cumulative, so the sixth round was the worst. Things were adding up: more neuropathy pain, more loss of appetite and weight loss, more bone pain, more sleepless nights, longer periods of neutropenia, more need for pain medications, more loss of muscle tone, more need for intensive 24-7 care. By the fifth round, the pain would last twelve or more days. Todd rarely got out of bed. He ate very little. His mouth and throat would be full of lesions from thrush. He just wanted to know when he could have more pain medications. I was terrified he would become addicted to them. He would ask me every day, "How many more days until it gets better?" I would usually answer, "Just a couple of more days," because I could never bear to tell him the actual number of days, as he would feel so discouraged if I did. His days just blended in a blur of pain and misery. Fortunately, he slept a lot. I would turn the television on to soft piano music, and that distraction seemed to help lull him to sleep. Todd is more of a Led Zeppelin type of guy, not soft piano music, but we just tried everything we could to help him deal with the pain.

Todd never said out loud, "Why me?" I did. A lot. It made me feel weak and guilty. While Todd told me a few times he wasn't sure how much longer he could take the pain, he never told me he was giving up. Seeing his strength made me stronger. At the hospital, I would hear Todd talking on the phone to people, and it always amazed me how positive and uplifting he was to friends and family. He made them feel better. One evening as I was sitting with him, he looked at me and said, "I never realized how much I'm loved." He was in awe of the friends and family who called or visited and the wonderful things they did for our family. These blessings continued day in and day out for many months. Golf buddies, our siblings, friends, our children's friends, pastors—they stuck with us. No one faltered; no one gave up. They just kept loving all of us.

So what is normal? Something I whined about while going through our nightmare was normalcy. I just wanted to feel normal again. "Normal" means different things to different people. I craved the ordinary. I would look at couples at stoplights and think, *Why can't we be ordinary like that?* I wanted to jump into the car with my husband and go grab a bite to eat. I wanted to run an errand on my way home after work. I wanted to wake up on Saturday morning with my husband beside me. For a year and a half, and at times today, I know we are no longer ordinary. But I have learned that doing normal activities really helps me cope. Washing the dishes, doing laundry, going grocery shopping—those things kept me sane. Those tasks were about the only things I could control.

Something that was most frustrating to me was losing control of my home. We had family, physical therapists, massage therapists, friends, and nurses in our home daily while

I was at work. I am very grateful for every person that helped me with Todd. There was no way I could have handled all that was thrown at us on my own. But my home began to not feel like my home. I would come home to furniture rearranged, someone else putting away dishes, someone folding laundry a different way. I felt as if I had no control of my space. Another part of my normalcy was now gone. We had so many changes to our lives in such a short amount of time. It started to feel as though I were sleepwalking through my life as so many other people controlled everything that happened to us.

Todd

April–June 2016

CHEMO ROUNDS FIVE AND SIX WERE A BLUR TO ME. I TOOK AS MANY pain pills as I was allowed. Marie was always worried about addiction, but the only thing I was addicted to was golf. My brother-in-law Peter's father was a well-known retired doctor, and he told me to take as many pain meds as I wanted! The biggest arguments Marie and I would have were over the pain medicine. Marie would not let me have a pill even if it was two minutes early. This would really piss me off. In fact it pisses me off thinking about it now as I write our story! But I know she did it out of love.

We learned the hard way how important physical therapy can be in the healing process, but it wasn't even considered by my medical team in the beginning. We had to learn that it's impossible for one doctor to be knowledgeable in all aspects of one's care, which is why there are specialists for everything. And remember: medical professionals *practice* medicine. the primary definition of practice on merriam-webster.com is "to perform or work at repeatedly so as to become proficient." I don't say this to criticize them; I say it to commend medical professionals. Because they are smart enough and brave enough to research and try new treatments and remedies, I am alive today. It took us a while to figure out why there were so many different specialists coming in to see me. It's because my oncologist was humble enough to admit he didn't know all the answers. He called on his colleagues to help him, which ultimately helped me. Overall, over twenty different medical specialists were involved in my care. Each of them took the time to carefully consider my case and treated me with kindness, respect, and empathy. I was a mess! But they earnestly wanted to help me recover and survive.

My body grew weaker and weaker with each round of chemo as I spent more and more time in bed because of the pain and exhaustion. As soon as we asked for physical therapy, it was ordered for me, and we learned it was very helpful. In hindsight, we should have asked for it from the first round of chemo. Therapists would come every day when I was in the hospital. By this point I couldn't get out of bed and go to the bathroom without assistance. We started with exercises in bed. Then, with a lot of assistance, I moved to walking. When I was at home, we had both physical and occupational therapists come a couple of times a week. I was adapting to a very weak body that I wasn't used to having. Occupational therapists worked on things like steps, types of chairs to sit in, checking our showers for accessibility, and identifying potential dangers in our home. Physical therapists worked on the actual body motions—simple things, such as raising my foot off the ground. I had developed drop foot as a result of the increasing loss of muscle, making walking more difficult. I struggled with simple exercises and often wondered whether I would ever again be strong enough to do these seemingly simple things. It pained me to watch Marie do physical things around the house. She never complained, but I knew it was exhausting her.

Rehabbing my body was a long phase of baby steps: moving out of a chair, standing for thirty seconds, taking a few steps with a walker, and so on. We set up a walking route in the house for me. At first I could take only one lap, then three, then five, then ten. I would go until the pain was intolerable, then rest and try again. This from a guy who less than a year before could walk eighteen holes carrying my clubs in a round of golf. The frustration of trying to do such simple, normal things was hard. This required internal determination that I did not know I was capable of. My family and friends would cheer me on to take a few more steps. I appreciated their support, but I felt so useless and defeated. When I was on outdoor walks, people would stop me to ask how I was, which I was grateful for, but I was afraid that while talking to them I would fall over or pass out and not be able to make it back home. Regaining strength was a slow process, but with persistence and a lot of hard work, the therapy helped get me back on my feet.

Going home was great, but we still had the worry of the cancer returning. Six weeks after coming home from round six, I developed a pain in my stomach located exactly where the malignant tumor and lymph nodes had been removed. Of course this occurred at 3:00 a.m. We rushed to the emergency room, where they determined the lymphoma had not returned, gave me some pain meds, and sent me home.

At 3:00 a.m. the next morning, the same pain returned. Back to the emergency room we went, where they once again determined nothing was wrong. Poor Marie was exhausted physically and mentally. What was going on? We decided to head over to the cancer center without an appointment, as the pain was worsening. By the time they worked me into their busy schedule, the pain was so bad I was in tears. I was desperate. The nurse gave me a dose of hydromorphone into my port. Hydromorphone is a *very* strong pain medication. One minute later, the pain was under control. I hugged the nurse as she giggled. Unfortunately, it was finally determined I had shingles. I thought to myself, *You have got to be shitting me! I've gone through a bowel resection, six rounds of chemo, gotten myself into remission and now I have shingles!* Sounds lovely, right? The shingles wrapped halfway around my lower stomach and lower back in a twelve-inch-wide band. The pain was constant, then sores developed, then they leaked pus, and finally they dried up. Nerve fibers were also damaged, and the pain continued for many months. All told, this lasted six months. Shingles can reoccur at any time. So far I've been lucky to not have had them again. *When will the suffering end?* I thought. It would not be for a long time. I was not even halfway through this nightmare.

Marie

January–April 2016

I WAS WORKING FULL-TIME, GOING TO THE HOSPITAL FROM WORK or directly home to care for Todd until it all started again the next day. Walking into the hospital each day was hard, but leaving Todd each day was worse. I would pack up my backpack, put on my coat, and kiss Todd as he lay in the bed. As I opened the door to leave, I always turned for one last look at him. It tore my heart apart each time.

When Todd was home, he was going to the cancer center at least every other day for blood work, blood or plasma transfusions, syncope issues, and such. As the chemo treatments progressed, it became difficult just to get to these appointments. Getting Todd bathed, dressed, and to the car was a slow and laborious process. Every time he stood, there was the possibility he would pass out, so I kept him sitting as much as possible. To get him down the hallway to the stairs, I would put him on a wheeled stool I had and push him to the steps. Then I would set him on the first step, get behind him, and slowly "walk" him down the stairs while clinching the gait belt I kept on him at all times. Getting him to the car took at least ten minutes of slow and careful steps and stops. Arrival at the cancer center meant going in for a wheelchair, getting him in it, pushing him into the building, parking the car, then going to retrieve him to check in for his appointment (all the while praying he had actually stayed where I left him and he hadn't tried to stand up).

After round five of chemo, I was close to a breaking point. As we sat waiting for our nurse practitioner, Tricia Yoder, to come in I wanted to lie down on the floor and go to sleep. Todd was in a continual fog of pain and wasn't talking much. It was very quiet as we waited. I could feel myself sinking as if I were sinking into sand. When Tricia came in, I was not my usual take-charge self. Tricia knew something was off. She asked whether I was okay. And I couldn't speak. I wanted to scream, "I can't do this anymore! I want it to be over. I want you to tell me when I will wake up from this nightmare. Give me back my husband!" But nothing came out. I felt terrible that she even had to ask whether I was okay. And I thought that if I voiced my real feelings, she might tell me the truth— that she couldn't tell me when, or if, it would ever end the way I hoped it would. Fear and weariness had overwhelmed me. So I just looked at her and said, "I'll be okay; it's just a really bad day." She just hugged me. Her job was to take care of Todd, not me. I still feel guilty about that day and have since apologized to Tricia. Her compassion that day was above and beyond. That hug pushed me through. I somehow pulled up my big girl pants and moved forward.

We will never be able to adequately thank our children and their spouses for what they did for us during Todd's illnesses. Our daughters and sons-in-law were right there with us as we met with many medical professionals. Each of them came up with questions I was too scared or stressed to put into words. They took care of both Todd and me. They took care of things at our home, including our dogs. I called my sons-in-law more than once in the middle of the night, and they never hesitated to come and help. They all interrupted very busy lives to help Todd survive. They scheduled themselves for shifts with Todd while I worked. I am sure that if I had been the one with Todd all day, every day, we may never have reached our thirty-sixth wedding anniversary! When they were concerned about something happening with Todd's treatment, they advocated for him. I kept a large binder that went everywhere Todd went so anything could be looked up if needed. I created an appointment worksheet for each person who took Todd to an appointment so everyone knew what happened and when. We were in constant communication about meds, blood work results, transfusions, and his general condition. We sent each other pictures of blood work results like most people send pictures of their dinners! All this might seem excessive, but it empowered each of us to confidently advocate best practices for Todd. And I believe that contributed greatly to our positive outcome.

Each of them saw their dad and father-in-law in ways one hopes a child will never see. They watched him get so weak he needed help with every step. They saw him in tremendous pain. They saw him cry. They saw him take so many medications we lost count. They saw him pass out. They saw the fear in his eyes. But most importantly, they never gave up on their dad. No matter how tired they were, how hard it was to miss work, how hard it was to watch Todd look weaker and weaker each week, how sad they felt, or how difficult all the scheduling became, they never once said, "No more." Instead they gave medications, helped him walk, encouraged him to eat and keep moving, entertained him, stayed with him when he was scared, and loved him deeply. Heck, Caroline even told him, "Hey, you wiped my butt when I was little; I'll wipe yours now if you need me to." That is big love!

Now, they did keep secrets from us—which is normally easier to do with Todd than me. But I was absolutely stunned to find out Katie had been admitted to the same hospital for a couple of nights in December 2015 with a Crohn's disease flare-up. I know I was very distracted with all Todd was going through, but it was so disconcerting to me that I was so distracted that I didn't see the signs. The good side of them keeping secrets is that Todd and I feel we have done a pretty good job of raising our girls to be best friends who will do anything necessary for our family. Knowing Katie was in the hospital would have torn me up inside as I tried to take care of Todd on one floor and Katie on another, not to mention feeling the need to help with the grandchildren as well.

Our grandbabies are the lights of our life. When Todd first became ill, Luke was three years old and Chase was just eight months old. Todd and I greatly missed the day-to-day interaction to which we had grown accustomed. Katie and Eric brought the kids to see Todd at the hospital whenever they could. It brightened our day so much when they visited. Luke learned very quickly about the ice-cream cups kept for patients. He and Todd shared many precious ice-cream parties on Pop's hospital bed! We also played some pretty fun games of hide-and-seek with the bed curtains and the closets in the hospital rooms. And the windowsills were perfect places to sit and watch cars drive in and out of the hospital and for playing with their little cars! But we missed out on a lot with the boys. That was an unseen and difficult side effect of cancer. While Luke was old enough to understand the basics and could talk to us on the phone or FaceTime with us, Chase was an infant. And sadly, we couldn't be with him as much as we had been with Luke when he was a baby. It took several months of visiting us at home as Todd recovered for us to get to know Chase again. It just plain ol' hurt my heart. Our patience paid off though, and now Chase doesn't remember not spending time with us. In fact, he gets a little perturbed with his parents when they pick him up from daycare (which is close to our home) and they can't stop at Re and Pop's. 'Cause there are treats at Re and Pop's. And Re and Pop never say no to treats!

Medical professionals are superheroes. They just are. Doctors, nurses, physician assistants, nurse practitioners, nurse techs, lab techs, escorts, housekeeping staff, therapists, food service workers, valets—these are just some of the people we encountered daily that did everything they could to make our medical crisis bearable. The hospital where Todd received his cancer treatments has made their number-one goal to "see" the patient, and that carried over to the caretakers as well. That may not be what they call it in their marketing plan, but it's what I saw and felt every single day.

Now, I know that we spent an inordinately long time over many visits (twenty-one inpatient hospital stays for a total of 141 days, many intravenous transfusion and fluid days, and hundreds of visits to the cancer centers) with these professionals, but every time we were there, the care was consistent. It didn't matter if it was a doctor, a registrar, a lab tech, or a nurse; every single person helped us through so many difficult days. I am sure that when some of them saw Todd and his medical reports, they couldn't be sure he would survive. But once they got to know him, I think they realized that Todd is a survivalist. Todd is very good with people (which is why he's a successful salesman), and I'm sure it helped that he wasn't too grouchy most of the time; but no matter how busy they were, each of them gave him outstanding care. And when Todd was in tremendous pain, or got a little down, they were there with empathy and a pep talk.

Todd's nurses and their techs were incredibly compassionate. Todd looked forward to seeing them—even though he knew he was going to feel like crap after they gave him his chemo. And they cared for me as well. They saw me trudge in and out after I had worked all day. They answered my myriad questions, asked what I needed, and never balked at heating up food or bringing me the items I needed to help Todd shower every day.

And the complimentary valet service the hospital provided—oh my, what a godsend. It sounds silly, but it gave me an extra fifteen minutes a day with Todd. I pulled up day after day, week after week, time after time, and the valets were all there with a smile. One day, a young valet who was especially kind responded to one of my comments about being back yet again that he was sorry that I had to be back. I briefly told him about Todd. He was clearly moved by our story and said he would be praying for us. From that day on, I had a friendly face to look forward to seeing. He took such good care of me. When he would see my keys hanging in the key box, since he knew the approximate time I left each evening, he would have my car waiting so I could get home a few minutes earlier. He was a prayer warrior for us, and he didn't even know us! I'm sure he was as kind to every other person he saw, but I think God sent him to take care of me. I never spoke to him for more than a minute or two, but I will never forget the compassion and love he showed this old, exhausted lady.

Glenn

May–June 2016

I AM A PASSIONATE MUSICIAN WITH A LOVE FOR PLAYING THE GUITAR. I played in numerous bands on the Sunset Strip in Los Angeles, even jamming with Slash from Guns N' Roses from time to time. My crazy partying lifestyle came to an end when I severely injured a finger. I began to focus on the audio side of music and now set up audio for some of the biggest stars in the biggest arenas around the country. I would best describe myself as a giving, excitable, funny, passionate, emotional person with a big heart.

I met my wife, Season, who is an incredible person, and fell madly in love. We had our first child, Errol, and we thought we were the all-American family. Little did I know how our life would change in early May 2016.

May 12, 2016

There's only one way for me to tell you this story, and that is for me to tell you all of it. The good, the bad, and the ugly. I'm sorry if any of this offends you, but it's the truth. These things really happened.

I've finally hit a wall. I'm a full-blown alcoholic and drug addict. How did I let it get this far? Season, my wife, is going to leave me, and I can't blame her. I've put her through hell. I need help, and I need it now! I call an addiction treatment center. They say the next opening they have is next week. When I tell my bosses, they are amazingly supportive of my decision to seek treatment. They even offer to keep me on the

42

payroll while I'm there so Season doesn't feel overwhelmed taking care of Errol and having to work.

My job takes me to Denver, then once I get home, it's straight to treatment. Thank God. I already feel a sense of relief just getting my dark, nasty secret off my chest. Maintaining this disease has turned into a full-time job. I'm starting to smell like I'm decomposing. I probably am. My liver is swollen, and I'm in constant pain. I know my body can't take any more, but I can't stop. How scary is that? I just need to make it through the weekend.

May 15, 2016

I have made it through work this week just fine. I can tell my coworker Noah is worried about me. He keeps trying to keep tabs on me since I told him my dirty little secret. I was kind of amazed how surprised most of my coworkers were when I told them that I was an addict. I guess I became quite the professional at hiding it. So of course on my trip back from Denver I justify rerouting my flight home to stop in Las Vegas for one last blowout. I already have the cocaine lined up for when I arrive. They even deliver it to my hotel room. How convenient, right? Right.

May 16, 2016

Well, this day hasn't started as I'd hoped. I stayed up all night drinking and shoveling cocaine up my nose with some unsavory characters. One of them is a hooker that I've become friends with in Vegas. It's not what you think. She's sick like me. We have quite the symbiotic relationship. She brings me cocaine, I pay for dinner and drinks, we stay up all night getting sideways, she goes and visits a client or two, then she goes home.

Last night was a little different though. She asked me for money to pay for her cable bill. I laughed at her, and she got really mad and stormed out fuming. I went to bed about 9:00 a.m. this morning. Now I am being shaken to consciousness in my hotel room by three or four security guards and a couple of Las Vegas police officers. What are they doing here anyway? Who let them in? I bet that hooker turned me out. There's no way out of this one. I'm done.

While answering questions from the police, I can't help but break down and sob. It's not an act. All I had to do was make it through the weekend, and I went down in flames. I hate myself. What kind of man am I? A good father? No. A good husband? No. A selfish drunk and a drug addict. Yes, that's what I am. One of the security guards asks me if I want to go to jail or the hospital. I tell him that I'm planning on going to treatment and I want to go to the hospital.

That night I wake up in the hospital around 10:00 p.m. And of course, Season is right there by my side. She took the first flight to Vegas once she found me. One of the nurses comes into my room and rattles off the laundry list of substances they found in my system tonight after I was transferred to a proper detox center. I'm now on a mandatory three-day psychiatric hold, which means the only way I leave before three days is in a body bag. Wow, I'm batting a thousand. I'm going home in three days.

Up to this point, these were the worst days of my life. I was a fully functioning addict, or so I thought. I had let Season down so many times that she couldn't take any more. She had been begging me to get help for about two years at this point. It turns out she was the one that called the police once she figured out I was in Vegas. She saved my life that day, and I try to thank her for that as much as I can.

My spiritual connection with the universe was gone. I was completely empty. The only way I could function was with drugs and alcohol. For the record, I've never used a needle. They scare me. One thing that I feel I need to emphasize is that there is a common misconception about addiction. There isn't a day that any addict wakes up and says to himself, "Wow, isn't this great?" You are so ashamed that you go right back to getting intoxicated so you don't feel the guilt anymore. Rinse, repeat. It's a vicious cycle that leads you straight to insanity. Every day is like a high-wire balancing act. I wanted to get help, and this was the night that got me there.

I have since gone back and thanked that security guard for being kind, compassionate, and insightful enough to send me to the hospital. Addiction is a health problem, not a criminal justice matter, and somehow he knew that. I believe that he was my angel that day. I guess you could say that this was the day I was "diagnosed" with my disease: addiction. The company that I kept during this time was shameful: drug dealers, junkies, prostitutes. I didn't care who they were; as long as they were going to endorse my disgusting behavior, then they were all right with me. They were like a pack of vultures picking a carcass clean on the side of the road. They were gone when I had no more money or drugs for them to take.

This brings me to another huge point about addiction that only addicts understand. "Birds of a feather flock together," as my grandad would say. You will surround yourself only with people who won't get in the way of you getting intoxicated. It's a sickening reciprocal relationship. You validate each other and somehow talk yourself into not feeling so bad about your behavior because the vultures are patting you on the back and doing it too. The shame that I feel when I think about those people makes me want to vomit at times.

However, there are times when I stand up in gratitude for those people showing me how sick I was. Growing up in Los Angeles, all I ever wanted was to be a musician. By the time I was twenty-one years old, I had been playing in a band on the Sunset Strip in Hollywood for a few years. I loved it. This would be my first introduction to excess drinking and drug use. By the time I hit thirty years old, I had long left Los Angeles, but the excess followed me. Addiction had its hooks in me, and they were deep.

May 24, 2016

I spend a few days in the detox facility in Vegas. I advise anyone to avoid this if possible. It's a humbling experience, to say the least. They strip you naked and make sure you're not "hiding" any contraband before they let you loose among the rest of the patients. They even take your shoelaces so you can't strangle yourself with them. The phone cords are about six inches long so you cannot hang yourself. You can't have any soap or toothpaste because they think you'll eat it to get high. You even have to dry yourself with a washcloth after you shower because they think you'll make a towel into a noose. I'm not going to lie; in my mind I was already dead, so finishing the job seemed to be a reasonable option. I was dead inside.

I share a room in detox with a kid that is on his third go-round in that little piece of hell. He is here this time because he heard voices telling him to kill his family. How am I supposed to sleep with this nut job three feet away?

May 27, 2016

I'm heading into treatment today. I'm excited about going to treatment, but I'm also terrified. I've been going hard for more than ten years, and I don't know anything else. How am I ever going to enjoy myself in social situations if I am not wasted?

Don't get me wrong; I want to be sober. I want to be the dad and husband that Errol and Season deserve. I'm just scared that it will not stick.

"God, help me please, because I can't help myself," I beg. Season and I say our goodbyes in the parking lot. I cry like a baby, and as usual, she is confident and strong, just like the day we got married! I said goodbye to Errol at home. That hurt. I feel as if I've failed him. I promised him that I would be the best dad that the world had ever known when I got back. I bought him a stuffed Minion from the movie *Despicable Me*. I'm glad that, at two years old, he probably won't remember any of this. God willing, he'll never know the horror of this disease.

My roommate is a guy in his fifties. This is his third time in treatment. That's the first thing I notice—this disease is indiscriminate. It affects every race, age, class, and gender. There's something comforting being around a bunch of guys just as sick as I am. They don't judge me, they just know what I'm going through; it's kind of like a secret handshake. Not the club I wanted to be in, but here I am. I am here for the right reasons. Time to make the best of it.

The first days in treatment are an absolute roller coaster. I feel good because I am eating three meals a day and am not feeding my body a toxic concoction of drugs and alcohol. Sometimes I am crippled by the sadness and depression that comes from withdrawal. I also feel hyperemotional because all the feelings that I've been numbing with booze and running from my entire life are now rising to the surface. I'm being honest when I say suicide seems like a reasonable option. I know what you're thinking: "But, Glenn, you have a beautiful wife, a beautiful child, a good job." And you're right, I have this utopian American dream life, at least on the surface. Internally I am a mess. Addiction drives you to the point where you can't trust your own thoughts. As I said, it's a cycle that leads you straight into insanity.

47

I cry a lot; we all do. I will tell you that one of the most beautiful things that you'll ever see occur in those treatment centers: twenty men between eighteen and seventy years old sitting in a circle and crying together. It's surreal. You have an instant bond and brotherhood with total strangers. You learn to trust each other and lift each other up. All we have is each other.

I cannot say enough about Season's strength and grace during this time. She only signed up to be a mother for Errol, but she has to be a mother to me as well. I'd nominate her for sainthood if I could.

It's ironic that Todd is being injected with "Red Devil" chemo to fight his cancer while the devil on my shoulder is killing me. In the deepest pain, we have no choice but to find ourselves. Please remember this. It will prove to be important later in the story. That's what we are setting out to do—find our true selves and lose the addict self.

Well, the rehab continues. Stuck in the looney bin. You thought I was really messed up? You should see some of these guys. Some of them make me look like a saint. I hate this place. I don't belong here. You can't have an iPod to listen to music. I can't possibly get through listening to these idiots for the next twenty-eight days.

There's a guy in here who is a meth addict. He told us a story in our process group that made me want to punch him in the face. He told us how he was scared to get out of treatment in a few days and have to face his son. His son is a meth addict too but is still using. Here's the kicker: this asshole introduced his son to meth. In fact, his son's first injections came from Dad. No wonder his kid is a junkie like him. What's that they say about the apple not falling far from the tree? Here I am, trying to get clean so I can be the best dad possible for Errol, and this guy is killing his kid.

I meet my counselor today. She seems like an old hippie.

She's super nice and compassionate, yet tough. She is a recovering addict who has dedicated her life to saving other addicts. I'd say that's pretty commendable. Maybe I'll do that someday. She tells me she came out of retirement because the addiction epidemic is so out of control right now that they can't find enough staff. There are all kinds of people in here, from wealthy businessmen to the run-of-the-mill junkie. I had no idea how bad the opiate epidemic is. The opiate addicts here started as heroin addicts. Now heroin is a second choice behind prescription pills. They crush them up and shoot them. It's hard to sleep some nights as the opiate addicts are in such bad withdrawal that they stand in the shower puking all night.

There is an older guy in here that is a classic alcoholic and was putting down a gallon of whiskey a day. I didn't know this was possible. His kids put him in here. He's super funny, unintentionally, with an old-school drawl. There's another guy in here I want to tell you about. He's a very young man, damaged like the rest of us, and has a baby due in three months. He's a sweet guy and was the first person to befriend me. We talk about parenthood. I told him the reason that I was in rehab was for my son Errol. God, I miss that little bugger. I also told him how profound becoming a parent was for me and that it inspired me to get clean. I can see the terror in this young man's eyes.

Calling home is heartbreaking. Season isn't very keen on talking to me right now, especially when I tell her that I want to leave treatment. Guess I can't really blame her. She puts Errol on the phone, and he tells me in his angelic voice, "I love you, Daddy." All I can do is cry when I hear him.

Did I mention the food in here sucks? It reminds me of an elementary school cafeteria. We have to be at "breakfast" every morning at 7:00 a.m. I pretty much just sit there shuffling the food around my plate until we're allowed to go back to our rooms.

I've been reading the AA book that they gave me when I checked in. It was written in the 1920s, so there's a little bit of interpretation involved. I feel like they're talking about me when they describe the behavior of an alcoholic—all the futile deals that you make with yourself like "I'll only drink beer" or "I'll only drink on special occasions" or "I'll only drink on weekends." Yeah, right. I've done everything the book describes to a T. I guess that's my confirmation that I do belong here. Season tells me that Errol is going to spend a week at my mom and dad's house. She deserves a break.

I did hate the first week of treatment. There is an arrogant quality to addiction that does nothing but keep you in that sickness. I thought that I was better than the other guys in there for a few days. That I wasn't as sick as them. Wrong again. I think the arrogance probably stems from the fact that I believed that I had fooled so many people for so long. Turns out the only person I was fooling was myself. Addicts do their best not to look inward. Everything is somebody else's fault. The arrogance quickly faded.

I learn to love my treatment process and the guys that are there with me. I come to be respected as a leader and example by the other guys and my counselor. Everyone carries a story, and even though our stories are all different, they all landed us in the same place. The counselors love to remind us of that fact. They'll tell us straight to our faces, "Your way got you here; why don't you give our way a try?" And they are 1,000,000 percent right. It helps that most of the counselors are recovering addicts. We can trust that they know exactly what we're going through.

I learned so much about myself in those first couple of weeks. Another point that I'd like to make about addiction is this: there is *always* trauma involved. What I mean is that every addict has had some sort of traumatic experience that is the driving force behind his or her disease, whether it be sexual abuse, emotional abuse, physical abuse, abandonment, death, or, God forbid, a mixture of all these things. Addicts don't use because they love to be intoxicated. We use because we are running from something inside. Usually there is some shame involved too. Listen up, boys and girls, here is one simple way to know if you're doing the right thing in your life: ask yourself, "Am I running away from something or running toward something?" Always run toward something—trust me. The thoughts and feelings that you run away from are not your fault, and they can be fixed. The biggest thing I have learned in treatment is that addiction is a brain disease. Treatment is 25 percent about chemical dependency and 75 percent about mental, spiritual, or emotional repair. The goal of any treatment program is to show you why you use the drugs and how to avoid those triggers.

I feel great after being clean for three weeks. I am finally able to identify and, most importantly, let go of the guilt and shame that triggered me to use. I am finally evolving into the man Season and Errol deserve. I have to say I'm proud of myself for this. Season saw the righteous, authentic, caring, and sensitive man that was inside when I couldn't see it myself. I have started to realize that I am, in fact, worthy of love and happiness. I'll say it again: Season saved my life. What an extraordinary person.

June 8, 2016

I am going on four weeks sober now. I feel incredible. I never thought that I could do this but now I know that I can. I've grown so much as a person. I have to go to the front office today because my insurance company is refusing to pay for me to be in treatment. What a bunch of garbage. The one time that I need to use my health insurance and they refuse to pay. Another burden of addiction is debt; this isn't cheap. I'd probably be dead if I weren't here. Where is the morality in that? I have to split the cost of treatment over two credit cards.

Things are looking up. Errol has been staying with my parents in Washington. The circumstances aren't the best, but there is nothing they love more than spoiling that kid. I talked to him tonight. He said that he was feeding apples to Sisco, the neighbor's horse. It still crushes me to talk to him. I miss him terribly. I guess you can say my disease is in remission.

June 9, 2016

This day changes my life forever. It was supposed to be just another day, and that's exactly how it started. Things were great, and I was finally seeing the light at the end of the tunnel. I might actually miss this place when I leave. It's the start of my last week in treatment. We have just gotten done with our physical activities for the day, and I'm showering before my process group when someone knocks at my door.

One of the guys says that Season just called and tells me to call home ASAP. I'm not quite sure what this is about, but I know something is wrong because she doesn't really want to talk to me much right now. I head over to the phone and call Season. "Hello," she says.

"Hey, what's up," I reply.

"Who are you with right now?" she asks.

"Nobody. What's going on?" I ask.

She starts sobbing and says, "I have to tell you something. There was an accident at your parents' house. Errol didn't make it."

I lose it, screaming "No, no, no, something is wrong! No, he's just a baby! He's my baby! No, my baby!"

My parents own a small general store in rural Washington.

My dad had gone outside to park a vehicle a customer had returned. Errol got out the door behind Dad. My dad went to park the truck and ran over Errol in the process. Errol was killed instantly. My dad picked him up and ran inside the house. He called 911 and started CPR with Errol lying on the kitchen table. He was already gone.

Just like that, everything in my world shatters into pieces. Everything that I've worked so hard for, gone. While I am on the phone with Season, the young man from before, my new friend in rehab, gets down on his knees behind me and prays. The house mom packs my belongings for me while I sob and wail. The last thing I do before I leave the treatment center is walk into the big meeting hall where group is in session. There are tears in everyone's eyes; some are sobbing. I stand in front of the entire group, holding a picture of Errol to my chest. I show them the picture and say, "This is my son, Errol. He was just killed in an accident. Please, take this treatment seriously, because this is what you stand to lose."

I leave the treatment center and go home to bury my son. When I get home, I go straight to Errol's room. I get down on my knees and just wail, pleading with God to take care of my son. He surely knows what it is like to lose a child.

Season is curled up in a ball, lying in our bed, dead silent. She is in shock. Imagine that feeling that you have in the pit of your stomach right now. Multiply that feeling by the highest number you can think of. Imagine that feeling never going away. Now imagine that you're still not even close to how it feels to lose a child. People tell you all the time that there are no words to describe it. I say there aren't *enough* words to describe it. It's the most desolate, lonely, confusing place.

● ● ●

Errol was everything to us. To this day, I've never had one resentful feeling toward my dad. He will carry that day with him for the rest of his life—a burden that no person should carry. Errol's funeral was beautiful. I remember the skies opening up and pouring just before it started. I remember thinking to myself that every spirit in heaven was crying for us that day.

Days turned into weeks and months. We were trying to move forward one day at a time. Season and I both started going to see trauma therapists. It turns out that we both have PTSD. That's not surprising.

Todd

July–September 2016

I CONTINUED TO GO TO PHYSICAL THERAPY AND GAIN STRENGTH AS summer began and my shingles healed. I was still in remission and feeling stronger week by week. In mid-July, we flew to MD Anderson in Houston, Texas. MD Anderson is considered by many to be the mecca of cancer research and treatments. The environment at MD Anderson is unique, with twelve floors of people with cancer challenges and outstanding medical professionals helping them. It felt a little like a haunted house, with numerous patients in wheelchairs looking weak and exhausted—including me! Dr. Bhatia suggested we visit an oncology lymphoma specialist at MD Anderson to see whether I qualified for any trial treatments in the event the lymphoma came back.

It was a shocking meeting. As the doctor reviewed my case, he drew and wrote on a piece of paper for about twenty minutes, showing us how my chromosomes (and a lot of other stuff that we did not understand) were not working properly. I finally said, "Doc, I am impressed with your knowledge, but I have no idea what you're talking about. Could you please give us the bottom line?"

The doctor said, "I took another look at all your tests, and you have been misdiagnosed … I believe you have diffuse large B-cell lymphoma."

"Sooo … again, what does that mean?" I asked.

"Well, your chances of lymphoma returning are very low, and you do not require qualification for trial treatments," he said.

"What about the treatment I already received; was that the right treatment?" I asked.

"Yes," he replied.

Marie and I were shocked and just stared at each other out of disbelief. You have to love the practice of medicine. After visiting professionals to help with my neuropathy and other side effects, we flew home. Again, God works in mysterious ways!

● ● ●

Note from Marie: "The bottom-line concerning Todd's diagnosis is that he received the proper chemo medications that brought him to remission."

● ● ●

This was a good reminder to us that medicine is not an absolute. It is termed "the practice of medicine." And aren't we all so very privileged to have people willing to practice medicine in spite of the unknowns and risks?

My upbringing in religion was sparse. My family would attend church services on Christmas and Easter. As a kid, I thought religion was boring. Raising a family of three boys, all my parents had time to do was separate us during our frequent fights! When Marie and I started hanging out, I saw that she and her family were active in their church. Her father was treasurer of the church, and Marie always enjoyed her church family, church camp, and mission trips. I had never experienced those things before. She had this purity and innocence and sweetness about her, as well as a love for the Lord. This was something I had never experienced. I felt lucky to meet her and date her, and I wanted to be around her for the rest of my life. Sometimes I think people think I was crazy when I explain this happened at age sixteen, but it is a feeling that I have never again felt. I distinctly remember the moment when Marie walked into our neighborhood grocery where I was working as a bagger and seeing her in the other checkout line, wearing a light lavender shirt and jeans, talking to the manager in her natural way, and the thought *Someday I am going to marry that girl* coming into my head. Honestly, I'm not even sure I knew what a girl was until then!

Early on as a married couple, we went to church inconsistently. I would play golf on Sunday mornings. As a teenager, my daughter Kelleigh read the entire Bible, and that left quite an impression on me. I thought, *She gets this, and I don't*. I tried to read the Bible a couple of times but found it difficult, and I didn't follow through.

This all changed when I was confronted with cancer. It became clear that unless I surrendered myself to God, I would die. I started reading the Bible, and Marie and I would pray together most evenings. I went to church when physically able and watched sermons on TV. Praying several times a day became routine. We have enjoyed attending Bible study classes together. I developed a personal prayer list. People praying for me had a huge impact on me. So many people I did not know would come up to me and say they were praying for me. When I was in pain, I prayed to God for relief. Often I could feel his warmth as he cradled me in his arms. I would be overwhelmed with God's love and then fall asleep.

Now that chemotherapy was complete, and we had been to MD Anderson, our focus returned to rehabbing my body. During August and September, I was able to improve to the point of hitting golf balls—poorly. I would sometimes fall down when swinging. I would sit in a golf cart, then stand and hit two balls, then rest again in the cart. Doing this was good physical therapy for me, but the mental health therapy it provided was even more healing. I could visit with my golf buddies, feel the sun, be outside, and enjoy the smells of freshly cut grass. What joy I felt being able to be outside after spending fifty-eight days as an inpatient through, at this point, twelve hospitalizations. All in a seven-month period of time.

At the end of September 2016, I woke up in the middle of the night with a fever, but by morning I felt okay, so I didn't say anything to Marie. The next night, the same thing happened. I knew something wasn't right, so I woke Marie up, and we decided we should head to the ER. I am so glad I did. They had no idea what was wrong and decided to admit me to the hospital. The tests began. They first thought it was something viral. I kept getting worse. Breathing became very painful and difficult, so they put me on oxygen. It was frightening how much it hurt to breathe. I was flat on my back, barely moving, gasping for each breath. I felt as if I had a heavy weight pushing down on my lungs. I didn't want to move because it was so painful. I could barely speak. I remember hearing so many things going on around me. I couldn't communicate to anyone about how I felt. It felt as though I were in a different world than everyone else. Dr. Bhatia told me later that I was close to death because all my organs were beginning to slow down because of lack of oxygen. The diagnosis we finally received was devastating. I had acute myeloid leukemia. The chemo I had received for the lymphoma most likely had caused it. The doctors were shocked, as they had never seen AML occur this quickly following chemo treatment. They considered an AML diagnosis five years after treatment as fast; mine showed up in five months. Even today they have no explanation as to how this happened. I had to wonder whether this roller coaster would ever stop.

During my struggle to breathe, I felt that I was enveloped by a soft white light and was cradled in God's arms, totally secure in his warming embrace. God was telling me I would be all right. I could hear my medical team and my family scurrying around me. But they had no idea God was holding me and letting me know I was going to be okay. I wanted to tell them, but I didn't have the energy to talk. I felt a tender connection with God I had never felt before, and I was at peace. He is truly the father of all of us. Hallelujah!

As I started my next round of chemo, I learned that a high percentage of bone marrow is in the sternum, therefore the AML was close to my lungs and was having the biggest impact on my breathing. I spent twenty-nine days in the hospital for round 1 of AML chemotherapy. The chemo side effects returned quickly. I still had pain from the shingles and had not fully recovered from all the other previous chemo side effects, and now I was getting more. It just seemed so unfair, but I knew feeling sorry for myself wouldn't help, so I told myself, "Let's move on, tough guy." The side effects were again awful. My ability to taste went away, I had thrush all over my mouth and throat, and I experienced extreme diarrhea, bone pain, joint pain, and vision and teeth issues. Some of my nails fell off my fingers and toes. And this was just after the first chemo round. My second round was only about a week away.

Marie

September 2016

SITTING IN THE COMMUNITY HOSPITAL NORTH ER, YET AGAIN, I was certain the lymphoma had returned. Todd had night sweats and a fever and was pale and listless. It was a helpless feeling watching the doctors and nurses try to figure out what was going on. Even though his CT scan came back clear, it was obvious from other tests that whatever was wrong was not good. Dr. Bhatia had the ER doctors admit Todd. And there we were again, on the MRO floor. Many of the same staff were still there, taking care of Todd yet again. The concern was written all over their faces. Todd lay in that hospital bed completely flat. Breathing was an incredibly difficult chore. He rarely spoke. We didn't have any answers. I was stressed beyond my capacity to even think clearly. I remember stepping out of his room and going to a back hall to call my doctor. I was going to need some anxiety meds to get through this.

I remember the exact moment Dr. Bhatia told us it was AML. I felt so defeated. How in the world were we going to do all this *again*? I was afraid to speak for fear I would completely lose control. I still get that stinging sensation of tears coming behind my eyes when I think about it. I mean, how much more could Todd take? How much more could our family take? I honestly didn't think I could do it again. But as I stared at the floor, willing myself not to cry, God tapped me on the shoulder. "You can do this, and you will," he said. I sighed internally. As I looked up at Todd, he, as usual, was all in and ready to fight.

The drive home that evening was tear-filled, and boy was

I pissed at God. I told him so too! I'm not sure whether I was depressed or experiencing shock after this news. I just went through the motions each day for a while. Food tasted like cardboard. Sleep was hit or miss. Fear was overwhelming. Thinking was foggy. But when I would get to the hospital each afternoon, there was Todd, positive and ready to beat cancer for a second time. So, remembering God told me I could do it, I got on board and did everything in my power to make sure he was successful.

Todd spent a month in the hospital for his first chemo round for the AML. We were back to our routine from the six rounds he received for his lymphoma. I was working all day, heading to the hospital to help Todd shower, make sure he ate a decent dinner, and catch up on all the medical reports of the day. I'll admit I really struggled through some of these days. It was very difficult to get up each morning knowing what my day held. I can remember savoring the first few seconds after I woke up each day when I hadn't yet remembered Todd had cancer again. And once again, I didn't know how much longer I might or might not have Todd with me. All his side effects from chemo came roaring back. Some days Todd was in so much pain that I would have to bathe him while he lay in bed. Thrush kept him from being able to eat much. He had diarrhea, syncope, neuropathy, and bone pain. I am amazed that he was able to survive the pain and agony yet again.

One evening Dr. Bhatia came in and told Todd his only chance at survival would be a stem cell transplant. Todd's blood cells showed damage that could not be healed. Without a transplant, the AML would return and take his life. This news made me feel as if someone had put cement in my shoes. A transplant sounded incredibly daunting. Inside I was so scared, but I couldn't let Todd see my fear. And Todd was his usual "Let's do this" self! We had to decide what hospital we wanted to pursue for the transplant. Going to MD Anderson would require a temporary move and me quitting my job where I held our medical insurance. That wouldn't work. After much consideration, we decided that St. Francis Hospital in Indianapolis was the best choice for Todd and our family. And so, with a lot of unknowns, naivete, and many fears, we started our third new journey in less than a year.

Todd

October–November 2016

AFTER MY SECOND CHEMO ROUND FOR THE AML, A CAT SCAN showed I was in remission. Miracle number two! These miracles were so merciful I wish I could have celebrated them more. I was just so weak I couldn't even do a touchdown dance. I have come to appreciate the special moments more as I have written this book. By this time, I had endured eight rounds of grueling chemo that each lasted for six to seven days. I had almost reached the lifetime limit allowed on one of the chemo drugs. I was lucky to go into remission after only two rounds of chemo. I don't think my body could have handled much more chemo abuse. The muscle and weight I had begun gaining over the summer were gone within a couple of weeks after my AML treatments began.

The doctors emphasized the importance of pushing myself to get in shape for my possible stem cell transplant—which was the only option to save my life. To satisfy the insurance company requirements, I would need to pass several medical evaluations and prove I was strong enough for the transplant, and a donor had to be found. A lot of things needed to come together! So now it was time to relearn walking again and to regain as much strength as possible so I had the best chance at qualifying. I needed to be as strong as I could possibly be to have the energy to survive the transplant. I needed to gain weight and muscle. Eating was always a problem, as the thrush in my mouth and throat affected my taste buds, and the sores made it painful to swallow food. When I walked, I was wobbly, and I couldn't walk too far without assistance.

Physical therapists visited the house three times a week. The therapists pushed me every day to do my best. Walking was tough. My drop foot was worse than ever, making it even more difficult. The nerves in my foot were compressed, making it difficult to lift my foot, causing it to drag. I had to restrengthen those foot muscles to lower my risk of tripping and injuring myself. Fall injuries can be fatal. I started doing laps on the inside of the house with a walker. From kitchen to dining room to living room to front hallway and then back to kitchen was one lap. Who would have thought we would all get excited when I could make a full lap! I started with one lap with my walker and eventually made it to twenty-five laps! Gradually I made it all the way up to walking outside by myself. I made it down the driveway and back up. Then I made it to the stop sign at the end of the street. I would finally walk a mile, which took about an hour. I could remember laughing at slow-moving old men when I was younger, and now I was laughing at myself! But I just kept going. I would see neighbors on my walks, and they would encourage me. Giving up was not an option.

Marie

June–December 2016

IN THE SUMMER OF 2016, TODD AND I STARTED THINKING ABOUT downsizing our home. At that point, we were hopeful that the lymphoma would not return, but we also knew that if it did, it would be a struggle for me to care for Todd in our two-story house, much less take care of our home by myself. We found a model home we liked and started seriously considering a move. But, of course, we were once again gobsmacked with Todd's second cancer diagnosis in September. We put everything on hold. Todd and I had some tough discussions after his AML treatments began and he was feeling better. I was at Community Hospital North after work one day and told him we needed to talk. At this point, we knew Todd would be an inpatient for at least a month, but we did not know whether he would qualify for a stem cell transplant. I had been doing a lot of soul-searching in the days after the AML diagnosis. Pulling myself together and thinking through the things I needed to consider was very difficult. But I knew that if I broke down and could not cope, it would be a horrible example to my children and even worse for Todd.

As I got ready for bed one night, I made myself contemplate what would happen if Todd did not survive this second cancer. None of us *ever* went there, because we were determined to remain positive. But I had to. I had to think about what my life would be like if we lost him. I had to envision him never coming home from a round of golf or a business trip, or simply having dinner with us. I had to think of family trips we would go on where we would all be without him. I had to think of going to our grandchildren's ball games alone. I had to think of the social times I wouldn't be involved in with our friends. But most importantly, I had to tell myself that I would be okay if I did lose him. I had to be okay for our family, but I really had to be okay for me. I didn't want Todd to carry any burden of worrying about me if this disease took him. That wouldn't be fair to him. So we had the hard conversation as he lay in his hospital bed with chemotherapy drugs coursing through his body. We talked about the what-ifs and the hope we had that those things did not happen. At one point he told me it was okay if I dated and found someone to love and be with. If I could put the emoji with big eyes and open mouth here I would! I appreciated that Todd told me it was okay, but dating for me was a hard no! By this time Todd and I had known each other for more than forty-nine years and had been a couple for almost forty years.

After we had that tough conversation, I realized I also needed to go ahead with our decision to downsize. I knew that whether I was taking care of Todd at home or not, we had a great need to be in a smaller, more accessible home and to simplify our lives. It was time to get rid of many of our belongings, reduce upkeep needs on a home, and concentrate on the truly important people in our lives.

And so, as crazy as it sounds (and it was crazy), we signed the documents to build a new house in December of 2016, just a couple of months after Todd was diagnosed with leukemia. I wasn't sure whether I was going to move into the house alone or with Todd, but I put my faith in God that somehow it would all work out. I am not a big risk-taker (ask our financial guy; I drive him crazy) but I knew in my heart this had to happen— and for more reasons than just being able to take care of Todd in a safer way.

We had raised our girls in our current home. We had thousands of memories of birthdays, cookouts, family, friends, boyfriends, holidays, and family time that were precious and warmed our hearts. Our girls were not overly happy that we had decided it was time to sell. But I had to admit to myself that I needed to leave this home so the next family could make heartwarming memories. My own memories of our home were becoming clouded with what can only be described as doom and gloom. For the past year, my memories were of me being alone in the house, wondering whether my husband would survive, or of me taking care of him at home every second I wasn't at work. With so many people in my house when I was at work, my home was being altered frequently—rugs pulled up to avoid tripping; dishes being put in different cabinets, medical equipment in our bedroom, the bathrooms, the kitchen, and our main living areas; furniture moved around to accommodate all of it. It finally came to me that "my" house was no longer my "home." Cancer had taken it. At that time, we had no idea about Todd's future. His final condition after a possible transplant was a big unknown. But I knew it had to be easier to take care of him in a house where I didn't have to pull him up steps using a gait belt! And while events relating to selling our house and finishing the new house were touch-and-go at times, it all worked out eventually (with a lot of help from many people) and proved to be a decision that gave me a lot of peace.

Todd completed his second round of chemo for the AML in mid-November. We were already scheduling appointments for his possible stem cell transplant. When I found out the transplant would not be until after the first of the next year, I panicked. Todd had no more chemo treatments scheduled. I knew his scans showed he was in full remission, but I was terrified that the AML would come back before his transplant, which would mean the transplant would not happen. Dr. Bhatia assured me the AML would not return, and blessedly he was right.

After spending Christmas 2015 at the hospital, we were grateful to spend this Christmas at home. I had decided not to decorate; there just wasn't time between caring for Todd, medical appointments and my job. Todd was discharged November 18, and we headed home. It was always nice to bring him home, but it was stressful at the same time. We arrived home to all the kids' cars in our driveway, so I knew something was up. When we walked in, we were greeted with smiling faces. All the Christmas decorations were up, and they had moved the furniture around to accommodate Todd's needs. This brightened our moods, and that Christmas spirit always holds a lot of hope. Our Christmas celebration was a bit quiet, as we knew that Todd would be heading to St. Francis for the transplant on December 28, but the fact that we were at home and together was not lost on us.

At our first meeting with Dr. Michael Dugan at St. Francis in mid-November, I felt as if my whole world was upside down and sideways. Todd had been through so much. And when one member of a family goes through something like this, the whole family goes through it in their own ways. We were all tired, frustrated, and scared, but we were fearfully hopeful that a stem cell transplant would heal Todd. We knew there was a long road ahead with no guarantees. Dr. Dugan asked Todd whether he wanted the chemo he would receive before the transplant to be an easier chemo or a more difficult chemo. The more difficult chemo would make Todd feel worse but could result in a better outcome overall. Todd asked the girls and I, and we decided together to go big so we'd have no regrets. I guess the good Lord made sure we knew enough to say, "Let's go for it," and not enough to say, "It'll never work."

Todd

FOR MY STEM CELL TRANSPLANT WE HAD DECIDED TO GO TO ST. Francis Hospital Indiana Blood and Marrow Transplantation. Located on the south side of Indianapolis, it is one of the top hospitals in the United States for stem cell transplants. This medical group has four doctors on rotation 24-7 and can care for up to seventeen patients in a dedicated wing of the hospital. In early November, we had an appointment with one of the transplant doctors, Dr. Michael Dugan, to begin the preliminary interviews and assessments to see whether they would accept me as a patient. Since my blood cells were no good, I would have to receive an allogenic transplant. I needed someone else's stem cells to live. Dr. Dugan agreed to take me on as a patient and asked me to do everything I could to strengthen my body in order to handle what was ahead. Our insurance had approved the transplant, and now we had to see whether my body was eligible for transplant. The search for a donor also began.

My brothers, Barry and Kent, graciously drove to Indianapolis from Ohio to be tested. One brother was a possible, but not ideal, match, and the other brother was not a match. Kelleigh and Caroline could be tested, but the St. Francis team wanted to go to the national and international blood marrow donor registries, Be the Match, and DKMS (German Bone Marrow Donor Center) before the girls were tested. And they found a person somewhere in the world that was a nine-out-of-ten match to my human leukocyte antigen (HLA) protein markers. HLA is used by your body to determine which cells belong in your body. The more matches, the better chance the body sees the donor cells as your own and won't reject them. This gives a better chance for a successful transplant. This match was better than my brother's match. The science of medicine is amazing. They then had to contact this person to see whether he was still willing to donate. The donor's answer was yes! That was miracle number three. Our family was so grateful to this person, a complete stranger, who was willing to try to help me. The donor needed to pass a physical and other testing, which he did. Marrow recipients are not allowed to know anything about their donors until one year after transplant, and that is only if the donors give permission. I was left wondering who this person was who was willing to try to save my life?

Marie and I spent an entire day in mid-December going from test to test at St. Francis. I had a breathing test, an echocardiogram, bloodwork, x-rays, and a bone marrow biopsy. I'm sure there were even more. The day was exhausting. Marie pushed me all over that hospital in a wheelchair because I just wasn't able to walk long distances. (Marie is good at a lot of things, but wheelchair pushing is not one of them! She ran me into more doorways, elevator doors, and corners than I can count.) But these tests were necessary to see whether I was strong enough to receive the stem cell transplant.

Marie, Katie, Kelleigh, and I met with Dr. Dugan later in December to see whether they felt I was medically strong enough to have the transplant. Dr. Dugan conducted some additional physical tests on me and then met with us as a group. He gave us a lot of information about what a stem cell transplant involves. He didn't sugarcoat it. There were no guarantees on what my outcome and my quality of life would be. He told me that if I stayed in bed and didn't try after the transplant, I would die. And he gave me a 40 percent chance of a successful transplant. Boy, the room sure got quiet at that moment. This was my *last chance* at survival.

My stem cell transplant was scheduled for January 5, 2017.

Glenn

December 2016–January 2017

IT'S DECEMBER 2016, AND WE'RE ON THE CUSP OF OUR FIRST Christmas without Errol. It's been six months, but it feels like six years. That ache in my heart never goes away—not for one solitary second. I've been going to therapy every other week in hopes of processing some of this grief. I'm still sober, by the grace of God. That's a miracle in itself, I believe. Dealing with the death of your child is complex. Season and I never both have a good day. Even if I have a "good" day, I end up feeling guilty about it. By "good" I mean not sobbing uncontrollably.

We're not going to do anything for Christmas this year. Things just aren't the same. I doubt they will ever be.

I got a call from DKMS (the donor registry) today. They said I'm a match for a leukemia patient who needs my stem cells. They asked if I would do it, and of course I said yes. They're going to fly me to a Seattle hospital for a physical and blood work. If I pass the physical, I'll be able to donate my stem cells. They won't tell me who the recipient is for a year after the donation. I'm so curious. It feels good to be able to help someone else, especially when I'm back to the familiar feeling of not being able to help myself. Merry Christmas.

● ● ●

I'm cleared to donate! I'm going back to Seattle again on January 4. They're going to do what's called a peripheral stem cell collection. I get hooked up to some machine that takes the blood out of one arm, spins it at high speed, separating the stem cells, and returns the blood to my other arm. Science!

• • •

The donation is complete. I hope it works out for the recipient. DKMS has been a great organization to work with. Truthfully, I'm surprised that I passed the physical after what I have put my body through. It's been a great experience so far. I wonder if I'll ever meet this person. I want to tell him how Errol saved my life and all the heartache we've been through. I also want to thank him for restoring some sense of purpose in my life. Losing Errol took every bit of my purpose away. I'm going to write him a letter.

Todd

December 2016–January 2017

On December 28, Marie and I drove to St. Francis Hospital to begin my transplant journey. It's about an hour's drive from our home. It was a pretty quiet drive. I was weak from my AML chemo treatments and an unexpected inpatient week in December at Community Hospital North when I came down with a fever and cold. But I'm pretty sure we were both thinking the same things: Would this transplant save my life? And what if it didn't? What quality of life would I have if it worked? The future looked daunting, to say the least. We knew that giving up was not an option, so we just pushed through.

St. Francis has an excellent reputation for stem cell transplant expertise, and the stem cell wing has its own air systems, water purifiers, door seals, and special cleaning teams. Anything you can think of to keep germs out and patients progressing in their recoveries is important. The four doctors at St. Francis Blood and Marrow Transplantation Unit use a rotation system that keeps all of them updated, and they all see every patient in their care. They meet weekly to share assessments, consider treatment, and discuss all of their current patients. This was so helpful when I went home, because we could talk to any doctor on call, day or night, and they were able to make sound decisions and recommendations to help me. Again I was blessed to have this hospital close to home and be accepted as a patient. Their nursing staff was also invaluable during my inpatient stay as well as my clinic visits. They always encouraged me and had a smile and kind words for me.

It was strange being admitted to the hospital when I knew I wouldn't be going home for at least a month—and that was if the transplant went well. On my first day of admission, they began preparing me for the transplant that would occur nine days later. A Hickman line was surgically inserted into my chest. The Hickman had three lumens (tubes) on it for all the different drugs I would need, including chemo, to completely wipe out any cancer hiding in my body. The process to prepare my body for the transplant started with six days of chemotherapy 24-7, followed by one day of rest. The stem cell transplant would take place on January 5, then I would receive two more days of chemo. The two additional days of chemo is something research hospitals have found increases the success rate of your body accepting the new stem cells. This would hopefully be my final chemotherapy treatment. That was a good feeling.

While my body was being prepared to receive the stem cells, the donor was traveling to an unknown hospital on January 4 to make the donation that just might save my life. His blood was going into a centrifuge to separate out the stem cells, and then his blood would be returned to his body during a six-hour process. The process was finished in the late afternoon, and the stem cells were frozen and given to a courier, who immediately took them to the airport. We had no idea where this was happening or who was willing to do this to save my life. We just knew that my transplant would take place at noon on January 5, 2017.

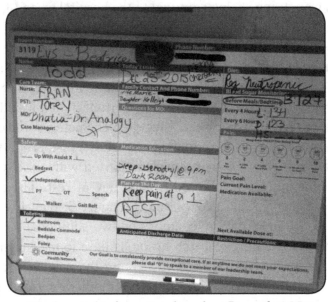

The hospital information board on December 25,
2015, with Dr. Bhatia's nickname of the day.

PICTURE CREDIT: MARIE IRWIN

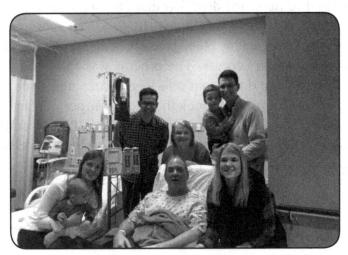

Christmas Day 2015 family photograph
at Community Hospital North.

PICTURE CREDIT: UNKNOWN

Todd and Caroline hanging out at
Community Hospital North.
PHOTO CREDIT: CAROLINE IRWIN

Todd after having his hair shaved off. His twelve-inch
scar is from his exploratory surgery in December 2015.
PHOTO CREDIT: MARIE IRWIN

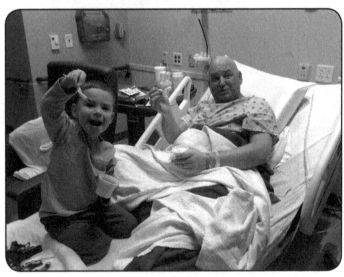

One of many hospital bed ice-cream
parties for Lucas and Todd.
PHOTO CREDIT: MARIE IRWIN

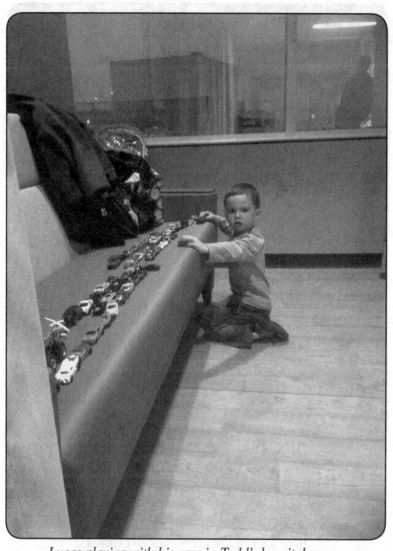

Lucas playing with his cars in Todd's hospital room.
PHOTO CREDIT: MARIE IRWIN

Todd with childhood friends Jim Gulick
(left) and Mike Murray (right).
PHOTO CREDIT: MARIE IRWIN

Marie and Todd on their way to MD Anderson Cancer Center in Texas.
PHOTO CREDIT: MARIE IRWIN

Bryan Mills with Todd at a golf tournament in September 2016.
PHOTO CREDIT: MARIE IRWIN

Todd and Lucas at the golf course.
PHOTO CREDIT: MARIE IRWIN

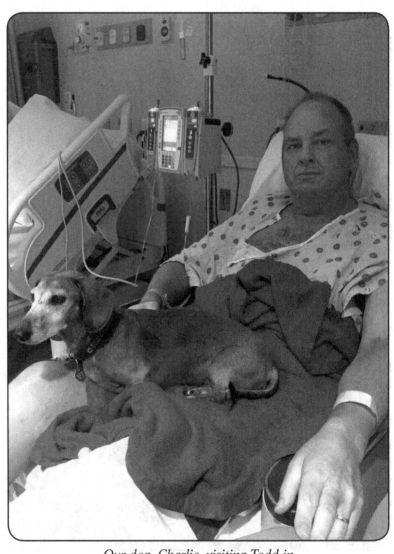

Our dog, Charlie, visiting Todd in
the hospital in October 2016.
PHOTO CREDIT: MARIE IRWIN

*Todd with his brothers, Kent Irwin
(left) and Barry Irwin (right).*
PHOTO CREDIT: MARIE IRWIN

Christmas Day 2016 at home. From top, left:
row 1: Eric, Drew, Kelleigh
row 2: Todd, Marie, Lucas
row 3: Chase, Katie, Caroline
PHOTO CREDIT: CAROLINE IRWIN

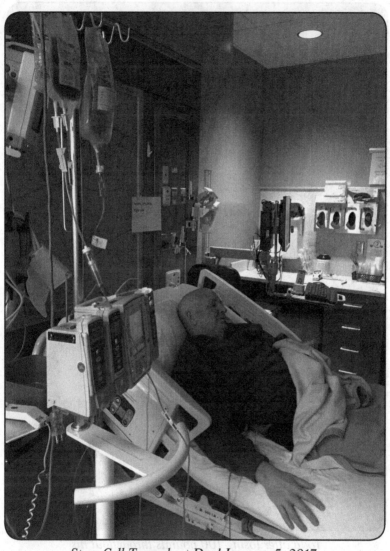

Stem Cell Transplant Day! January 5, 2017.
PHOTO CREDIT: MARIE IRWIN

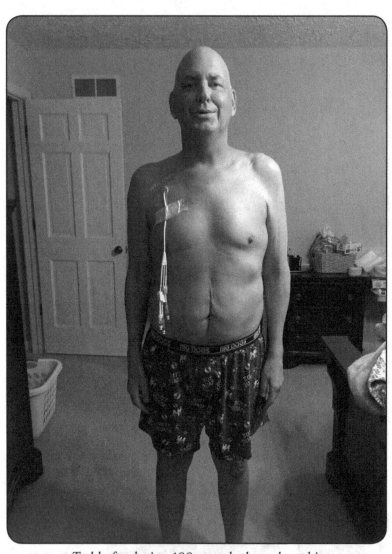

Todd after losing 100 pounds throughout his
cancer treatment and stem cell transplant.
PHOTO CREDIT: MARIE IRWIN

Todd at home with Chase and Luke during
recovery from his stem cell transplant.
PHOTO CREDIT: MARIE IRWIN

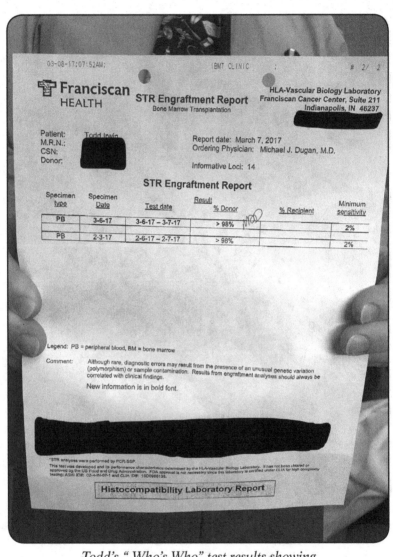

*Todd's "Who's Who" test results showing
he would survive after his transplant.*
PHOTO CREDIT: LYNN PONT

Todd happily finishing last at The Michael Treinen Foundation Turkey Trot in 2017.
PHOTO CREDIT: MARIE IRWIN

*Todd and Marie with Elliott, Season, and
Glenn Thornton in Boise, March 2018.*
PHOTO CREDIT: CAROLINE IRWIN

The Irwin family with Todd's donor,
Glenn Thornton, in Indianapolis.
PHOTO CREDIT: UNKNOWN

At the beach in 2021. Left to right: Drew, Caroline, Kelleigh, Marie, Todd, Sam, Chase, Emily, Katie, Luke, Eric.

PHOTO CREDIT: CAROLINE IRWIN

ON THE EVENING OF JANUARY 4, I SAT WITH TODD IN HIS SEALED-OFF room. Outside it had started to lightly snow, and it would continue to do so through the night. I was dreading the hour-long drive home, knowing I had to be back at the hospital in time for the transplant. Members of our church care team were planning to visit and pray with us the next morning. When Todd realized it was snowing, he began to talk me into staying at a hotel close to the hospital. After a while, I realized that it was a good idea and quickly made a reservation. (Remember: I kept a fully packed suitcase in my car for over two years, so I had everything I needed!) This allowed me to stay with him a while longer, and we began talking about what was to come. Of course, we didn't really know what was to come, but we tried to prepare ourselves for everything. Neither of us said anything about Todd not surviving; it wasn't an option for us. In fact, a few days before the transplant, I started a needlepoint belt (which are very popular in the South) decorated with logos and symbols of the Ohio State Buckeyes for Todd. It was a good project to work on during the many hours in the hospital. And it was a little bit of me saying, "You all just watch Todd; he's going to survive and wear this belt!"

When I arrived at the hotel that evening and checked in the desk clerk told me that my room had been paid for. My sister, Mary, somehow figured out where I was staying and paid for my room. What a warm feeling of love and support on one of the most stressful nights of our ordeal.

Todd

January 2017

MY MINDSET AT THIS POINT REQUIRED A LOT OF FAITH IN GOD. JUST trusting and surrendering to him was my strategy. I knew this was probably my final chance of surviving. When you consider all the miracles our God has performed for me, it is just logical to follow your faith. His spectacular miracles are everywhere if you just look for them.

My donor's stem cells arrived at the hospital very early on the morning of January 5. In fact, they arrived so early that the phlebotomy department processed them and had them ready to go two and a half hours early! Marie was at the hotel, expecting the transplant to begin at noon. When my nurse told me the transplant had been moved up to 9:00 a.m., I called her immediately. She quickly packed and got to the hospital with about thirty minutes to spare.

As the medical professionals that administer the transplant began to gather in my hospital room, each one of them commented on how great the donor's stem cells looked. They were all very excited. Of course, Marie and I really had no idea what they were referring to, but it made us happy that they were happy!

The actual transplant bag of stem cells looked like a good, thick marinara sauce. It was connected to the Hickman line lumen, and in it went. A transplant sounds very complicated, and it is once it's inside your body, but the actual process of getting the stem cells into my body was a bit anticlimactic. Thank God! The entire process took about three hours. After one hour, my body started shaking uncontrollably, and I got very cold. This extreme cold ignited my bone pain, and I could not stop shaking. The nurse gave me some meds to help the pain, but I felt miserable for several hours. The coolest part of the transplant is that it's sort of like an oil change (a very expensive one)! Eventually my blood type would change to the donor's blood type. That was fine with me, because at this point I knew my own blood was useless.

The chemo I received before the transplant was designed to completely kill any remaining bad cells, but in doing so it wiped out my immune system. After the transplant, the doctor explained my immune system would redevelop as if I were a newborn. I would require receiving every immunization I had received during my first two years of life on the same schedule as an infant. I also had to be extremely careful about germs. For the first thirty to forty days after the transplant, I could see only doctors, nurses, and my wife. When anyone was in my room, he or she had to wear gowns, masks, and gloves that were changed every time the person left the room. I rarely saw a full face, which was a little disturbing. I couldn't see smiles or expressions on people's faces. This reminded me daily why I was in that room. Except for a few walks in the hall prior to my transplant, I did not leave my room for nineteen days.

It was a little like what I imagine solitary confinement would feel like. I had no routine, calendar, or normal existence. There was a total of about fifteen people that came in and out of my room during this time. I felt like a science experiment. They were trying all kinds of things to help me. I was completely dependent on them for my survival. The room wasn't very cheerful. It was very sterile. It was January, and it was gloomy, with there rarely being any sun. Reading or watching television was difficult because of the side effects I was having, including difficulty concentrating. There was no fresh air from the outdoors. And honestly, the only thing I gave a shit about was myself. Was I going to make it? My world was the only thing that mattered. I was sad sometimes. There was nothing to look forward to. I was isolated from the outside world, and my body was full of drugs. It was bleak. I had no plans, no job. I didn't know or care what day of the week it was. I felt lost in space.

The side effects from the chemo hit about a week after the transplant. The fatigue, muscle pain, brain fog, thrush, and diarrhea all came back. I had reached nine rounds of chemo treatments by now, and my body knew it! My diarrhea was at its all-time worst, and I didn't have the strength to even get out of bed and make it to the bedside toilet, much less the bathroom. By the time I hit the nurse call button and she suited up to come into my room, I had already pooped myself in the bed. The nurses had to start using adult diapers on me and were a bit frustrated with me. They thought I was not trying hard enough to hold it. But I wasn't allowed to get out of bed by myself; an alarm would sound if I did. It was *The Shit Game Show*, hosted by Stem Cell Transplant, and I was the only contestant—and I was losing! I got a little testy with a couple of the nurses, but we finally worked through it, and my diarrhea improved after about a week. I recall one nurse saying that eventually she would get here in time to get me out of bed and that even if I pooped on the way to the bathroom— which I did—it would be progress. I eventually won *The Shit Game Show* gold medal!

Marie

January 2017

THE MIDDLE OF JANUARY WAS NOT FUN FOR MANY, MANY REASONS. Driving to the hospital every afternoon was not fun. The cold, sometimes snowy, walk into the hospital was not fun. Wearing all the safety personal protective equipment (gown, gloves, and mask) was not fun. But the most "not fun" was Todd! He was so miserable dealing with the chemo and transplant side effects. I would take a really deep breath and try to find some positive energy before stepping into his room each day.

On January 14, I walked in and he was in a very crabby mood. This was not normal for him but was certainly understandable. He had been put in adult incontinence underwear because he had basically told the nurses he wasn't going to try to make it to the bathroom when he was having diarrhea. The diarrhea was happening so frequently that he was just done with it. I knew I had to figure out how to motivate him to push through yet another hurdle. I, too, was tired of all the hurdles by this time.

Something that Dr. Dugan told us at one of Todd's evaluation appointments echoed in my brain often. He told Todd that if he didn't get out of bed during recovery, he would die. It was a fact. So I knew I had to try to motivate Todd. I started the conversation by reminding him that the faster he could control this, the faster he could go home. He didn't buy it. He hadn't seen our children or grandchildren since late December, and I thought surely that would entice him. Nope. He was not having any of it. So I lit into him about how he wasn't trying hard enough and he was letting all of us down. Well, that really pissed him off! And we were off to the races in an extremely

99

rare, for us, quarrel. We really don't argue very much, but this argument was a doozy! After some heated exchanges and a bit of voice raising, I grabbed my purse and walked out of the room. I was done and so over *all* this. I stormed off the transplant floor, and I think steam was coming out my ears while I waited for the elevator. I just walked blindly all over that hospital. After I calmed down, I went back up to the transplant floor and just sat in the waiting area. My phone rang; it was Kelleigh. Knowing she didn't know what was going on, I answered. But she did know what was going on—because Todd had told her! Now I was *really* pissed off! I stormed back into Todd's room (as much as I could, anyhow, after having to stop and put on all the PPE). We had a few more words and determined I should go home. I felt I had said what I needed to say, and I also knew that sometimes Todd needed to be challenged into doing some things. We weren't going to come to any agreement, and we both needed space. I thought the subject was closed.

But it wasn't. I got home, and my phone rang. It was Dr. Dugan. I immediately thought it had to be bad news. "Hello," I answered.

"This is Dr. Dugan. I heard that you and Todd had a pretty big argument," he said.

How in the world did he know this? I said that we had. We talked for about ten minutes and I told him that having known Todd for as long as I had, I knew how to motivate him. And while I had been very upset, I felt sure it would push Todd over the hump to help himself more. And I was right. Todd did see that he was beginning to give up, and his fight came back. I still have no idea how Dr. Dugan found out about our fight. I have a feeling the nurses may have had their ears to the door and ran when they knew I was heading toward it! I'm still a bit embarrassed!

Todd

January–February 2017

I WAS FINALLY ALLOWED TO GO HOME AFTER SPENDING TWENTY-seven days in the hospital.

As I sat in my wheelchair at the hospital entrance waiting for Marie to get the car to take me home, a kind lady walked up to me and said she wanted to tell me something special. She explained she'd had three brain cancer surgeries and that during the third surgery she had a moment when God told her she would be all right. The Lord then told her she would run into me, and she was to tell me I would be okay as well. She smiled at me with a smile I will never forget and walked away. I believe she was an angel. I was frozen with wonder. Marie pulled up and pushed the wheelchair to our car. I told her the story, and she stared at me. Her face was shocked and happy all at the same time. What else could we say but "Praise the Lord!" We sat there with tears streaming down our cheeks.

I was finally home, and it was time for my rehabilitation to begin for the third time. I still could not be left alone, and we could not ask our friends and family to help anymore; they had done so much already. Marie hired a private nurse, Lynn Pont, to take care of me at home while she worked. Lynn is an angel. She saw me at my worst and would always help by staying positive and pointing out my small improvements. Besides the normal side effects, I had incredible back pain from the high amount of prednisone I was taking, which was causing a great deal of muscle pain. Constant back massages (and I mean *deep* massages) were required, as the pain was unbearable, and I could not sleep. At night I had to sleep sitting up in our bed due to the pain. Thank goodness we had an adjustable bed to raise my head. Lynn spent a lot of time giving me massages, listening to me moan while she used her sharp elbows to knead the knots in my back, and watching *Law & Order*. It was my favorite show. As our daughter Kelleigh noted, we all spent a lot of time watching *Law & Order*! The antirejection medications were having me do some strange things as well. I was told that I would feed myself nonexistent food that I plucked from the air. I was constantly falling asleep, and people were trying to wake me up. I would make odd movements with my arms. We had no idea why I was doing these things. People didn't know whether they should laugh or cry! And I had no idea that I was doing these things.

KNOWING THAT TODD COULD NOT STAY ALONE ONCE HE WAS released after his stem cell transplant, the family made the decision to hire a private nurse to be with him each day while I worked. While it was a very expensive decision, we all felt it was the right one for our family. There was no way we could expect our family, immediate or extended, or our friends to stay with Todd for eight hours a day as well as take him to his many appointments over an hour away from our home. Our son-in-law Eric knew a former colleague that might be interested and contacted her. We were blessed to have Lynn Pont take care of Todd. The school system I worked for was gracious enough to allow me to come to work thirty minutes late each day. Lynn came at 7:30 a.m. each morning and stayed until 3:30 p.m. We still had to find daily coverage for Todd for about thirty minutes until I could get home from work a bit before 4:00 p.m. The kids and many friends helped out, and I am so grateful for each of them being so willing to entertain and stay with Todd.

On Lynn's first day, Todd had one of his regular appointments at the St. Francis Cancer Center. I went with Lynn and Todd that morning to help acquaint Lynn with the staff and the protocol at each appointment. While we were waiting to see the doctor, Todd's transplant coordinator came into the exam room. She had tears in her eyes. Immediately I panicked inside, thinking there was something wrong with the stem cells Todd had received. But Vickie told us Todd had received a letter from his donor. We were stunned. While the donor and recipient can't talk to each other or meet for a year after transplant, they could communicate through letters. Vickie handed me the letter, saying she had never received such a moving donor letter. The letter had all personal information redacted. This is what I read:

Dear Recipient:

My name is ███. I hope you're doing well considering the circumstances. I'm sorry that you're going through this but you should know that you have an army of people, mostly strangers, on your side. How beautiful is that? ████████ and her team are bad asses. I don't know who you are, and truthfully it doesn't matter to me. When ████ and ███ called and told me that I was a match for donation I knew that it had to be done. I would hope that anyone that got that call would do the same. I have no doubt in my heart that you are truly grateful for my donation, but I wanted to take a moment to thank you. You don't know this, but you helped me too. On ██████ my beautiful 2½-year-old son, ████ was killed in a random and tragic accident. He was everything to my wife and I. It probably comes as no surprise that it was, and still is, a horrible, heartbreaking experience that I wouldn't wish upon anyone. I never knew that I could cry so hard or feel a pain so deep. I've spent every waking second since his death searching for answers and wondered how I could possibly go on living without him. How was this just? How was this fair? Why him? I've truly never felt such darkness. Then, a couple of days after ██████ birthday, ███████ called with the news. I was a match for someone who needed help. I said "yes" right away. As we went through the verification process the darkness that had been dominating my life started to turn to light. Maybe I was actually going to make a difference. Maybe I would start losing the hopeless, helpless feeling that I couldn't give away. And then ███████ called again. "It's confirmed," she said, "you're all clear to donate." "Let's do this," I replied. And we did. Next thing I know, I'm on a plane to ███████ and the rest is history. At long last, a light in the dark! I don't know how to explain it, but this universe that we live in works in mysterious ways. I guess all that I'm trying to say is "thank you" for letting me be a part of this. You've given my wife and I a light in the dark. I hope the very best for you and your family. I'll never forget this experience, the human experience.

███████

My eyes filled with tears. "Wow" was all I could say. I passed the letter to Todd. My heart filled with pain for the loss of their child. And then to see the courage they had to help a complete stranger was astonishing. How could we ever adequately thank them for showing us such kindness. Todd passed the letter to Lynn. We all sat there a little stunned. I couldn't wait to share it with the girls. We had talked occasionally about the donor, wondering where he or she lived, whether he or she was a man or a woman, and how we hoped we could one day thank him or her. Now we could at least send the donor a letter. Each of the girls and I did just that. Todd was not able to write or think very clearly because of the antirejection medications and wasn't able to send a letter. Plus, secretly I think he just wanted to speak to the man that had saved his life. We extended our deepest condolences for their loss and gratefulness for their compassionate act to help Todd. The girls told Glenn about their dad and what his survival meant to us. We hoped that Glenn and Season would feel the good they had done and that maybe the darkness would get a little brighter. And we hoped that in eleven months both Todd and Glenn would agree to contact each other. Here is the letter I sent to Glenn:

Dear Donor,

Thank you for your letter. It had to have been incredibly difficult to write and we want you to know that it touched us all very deeply. You have been in our prayers since the day we were told they had found you as a possible donor for my husband. We were amazed at your generosity and kindness from that first day. Now that we know a little more, we are in even more awe. Your loss broke our hearts. We cannot imagine the pain and grief you are feeling. We will continue to pray for you and your wife.

Receiving the news that a donor had been found was a joyous day for us. It gave my husband and our family a chance at life. We also felt a little trepidation as well. We knew how long the journey would be, and what a long journey we have already experienced. My

husband has experienced two cancers and now
the stem cell transplant in less than a year and
a half. And your generosity has given him the
chance to regain his life and livelihood. He
is slowly recovering and is doing well from
a medical standpoint. Your badass medical
team and our badass medical team have really
rocked this transplant! We hope and pray that
my husband's recovery will move forward with
few problems. For now we take it day by day.

Your generosity of your stem cells, time and
desire to help—all while experiencing your
unthinkable loss—is inspirational. I will always
use you as inspiration as I move forward in life.
I'm sure you have many thoughts, like we have,
of why this happened to us. But God is always
there for us and will guide and care for us, even
in our moments of anguish and pain. God's
blessings to you and yours. Please know that
our gratitude to you is unending.

With much respect,

███████████, the recipient's wife

We hoped we would get to meet Todd's donor as soon as
we could.

Todd was going to the clinic at St. Francis every other day
or so at this point and would continue these visits for several
months. Some days I would have to have him ready to go
directly into Lynn's car for an early appointment. Getting both
of us ready to be out the door by 7:30 a.m. was crazy. Todd
could not shower, dress, or get downstairs by himself. It was

like having a 175-pound toddler at times! His antirejection medications made him a little looney—well, a lot looney! I would turn my back to grab something, and he would be grabbing for nonexistent apples in the air or trying to stand up without assistance. He struggled with forming thoughts and talking. He didn't make a lot of sense at times. His hands trembled, making it difficult for him to dress and eat. He was so weak that I would put him on a medical stool with wheels and roll him to the steps. I kept the gait belt on him all the time again in case he tripped or started to fall so I could grab him. I would sit him on the top of our steps, get in front of him, grab the gait belt, and slowly make our way down the steps. I kept his downstairs walker at the bottom so I could grab it and then make our way to the family room. His diarrhea was still a problem, and he often couldn't make it to the bathroom. We still have a pair of shoes that were bleached several times after accidents. We call them "the poop shoes"! He was still passing out on occasion, and we never knew when it was coming, so we had to always be prepared and present. These days were often long and exhausting. And sometimes our nights were just as long.

One night was very trying. Todd was using the bedside toilet at night for safety. I heard him get up and move to it, and I drifted back to sleep. And then there was a crash and a yell. As I rounded the corner of the bed, Todd was lying on the floor with a gash in his forehead, and poop was everywhere! He had gotten dizzy trying to stand and had pulled the toilet over as he fell. For a second, I just froze. This was not what we needed at 2:00 a.m. Todd was conscious, and once I assessed his forehead and knew he was okay, I just surrendered to a long night of cleanup. I got him into the shower and onto his shower chair, and I stripped the bed and remade it while he cleaned up. Once I got him back into bed, I started on the furniture and carpet. I know I cried a couple of times. Two hours later, I laid back down only to hear my alarm go off an hour later. Time to start another day.

Lynn was so kind and patient with both of us. She probably still thinks I was a crazy lady because of all the information and instructions I gave her every day. But she was always receptive and kind as I went through my list each morning. When Todd was so out of it on his medications and we were so afraid he wouldn't come back to us, I left homework for him to do! I made him do everything from third-grade math problems to writing our kids' names over and over. I also made him do word searches. (Though I made them about sports so he would enjoy them, he still hated doing them.) Todd also struggled with staying awake during the day. And I needed him to sleep at night so he would let me sleep. In the evenings, I would stand in front of him, holding his hands, moving his arms, and talking to him to keep him awake. At night I sometimes tearfully begged him, "Please let me sleep!" There were many days when I was going on three or four hours of interrupted sleep. Not fun!

Lynn made sure he received his medications (he took them four times a day at this point), ate and drank enough fluids, and did his physical therapy. She took him to countless clinic appointments that sometimes lasted all day when he needed transfusions or IV fluids. Sometimes she had to leave Todd at the clinic, and I would race down there after work to pick him up before they closed because his appointments lasted so long. She filled out my clinic appointment forms I created so I would know everything that happened. And she also called me at work one day and gave me some of the best news I have ever received.

On March 8, 2017, Lynn called my cell phone while I was at work. For some reason, that day I was out of the school office and in the primary wing of the school. When I saw who was calling, it scared me. I quickly popped into a first-grade classroom that was empty. I grabbed a piece of scrap paper because I was afraid that I would not be able to remember what she said. Lynn immediately allayed my fears, saying she had good news from Dr. Dugan. She said, "He's going to live." I was not prepared for this information to come from this appointment, and I burst into tears. Lynn said Dr. Dugan had told her that Todd was in molecular remission. That was the news we had prayed to hear.

Just as our conversation was ending, the classroom teacher, Audrey, walked into the room. I was crying, and she immediately came to me. It was all I could do to tell her that I had just found out that Todd was going to live. She gave me a big hug. I wasn't sure what to do. I knew I couldn't go back to the office in my current state, and I knew I had to tell the kids this wonderful news. I went into one of the vestibules and called each daughter to tell her that her dad was going to be okay. As I look back on this day, I am so grateful to Lynn for calling me. I am not sure I ever believed Todd wouldn't survive—we just never let ourselves go there—but considering Dr. Dugan had given him a 40 percent chance to live, maybe we should have. Lynn was such a comforting help to us all; we were truly blessed she was available and willing to care for Todd.

After Todd started his stem cell recovery, I took some tote bags full of items that had become a staple in my own hospital bag to the Community MD Anderson Cancer Center North for distribution. They had opened a brand-new building, and I noticed that it provided valet service. I knew how helpful that was to cancer patients and their caregivers. I ran in with the load of bags, dropped them off at the information desk, and headed back to my car, which I had left parked at the far curb. My eye caught a glimpse of the back of a red shirt (like the valets wore) and a head of dark hair. Remember the valet that took care of me? I thought there was no way it could be him. But something made me stop and poke my head in and say his name. He turned around and exclaimed, "It is you! I saw your car; is everything okay?" I told him that Todd was recovering from his stem cell transplant but it looked as if it was all going to be okay. We gave each other the biggest hug, and I got to thank him for all his kind words, his taking care of me, and especially his prayers. I found out much later that he was a part-time youth pastor and worked at the hospital to make ends meet. I hope he knows how his kind heart helped a tired, scared old lady.

Todd

February 2017–January 2018

THROUGHOUT MY RECOVERY, THE DOCTORS RAN AN ENGRAFTMENT test they called "Who's Who." It was just what it sounded like. It measured the percentage of stem cells in my blood that were mine versus the donor's. They hoped the test would find the stem cells were 90 percent or more the donor's. They ran the first Who's Who test in early February, and the results were 98 percent donor. This was very good news. The doctors had also explained to me that one of my chromosomes had been damaged by all the chemo and that it was important for the new stem cells to heal this chromosome. A test for this was also run, and it confirmed the chromosome had been repaired. This was miracle number four. After learning these two things, I thought I just might survive this incredible fight! This was the moment when I *believed* the worst was over. As I look back, I see that I was right!

My memories of February through March are spotty. The antirejection medications made me do some very strange things. I don't really remember doing them, but plenty of people have told me the odd things I did. My body ached, I had trouble sleeping, the diarrhea was never-ending, the neuropathy made it difficult to walk, my bones ached from the chemotherapy, most foods tasted terrible, and I continued passing out on occasion. This period was a monumental struggle. And not knowing whether my quality of life would improve enough to allow me to enjoy my family and support them made this one of the most difficult times of my journey. One day, one of the doctors told us that it was important that we not look for day-to-day improvements but rather that we look for week-to-week changes. This proved to be very helpful when I would do something and think, *Wow, a week ago I couldn't do that!*

Marie's family had a miniature dachshund named Dixie when she was growing up. I thought Dixie was a pain in the ass. Caroline was nine years old when she called a family meeting where she presented a chart of pros and cons of three breeds of dogs and a chart of why we needed a dog. I wanted a Lab or a retriever, but Caroline's choices were a Jack Russell terrier, a dachshund, or a beagle. Marie, of course, wanted a dachshund, and the girls all agreed with her. We ended up with a little black one and named her Gracie. Gracie was a great dog and was loved by all of us. When Marie went back to work when the kids were older, she called me and said that she wanted to get another dachshund so Gracie would not be lonely. I didn't like the idea but was once again overruled. I debated with Marie and the girls and at least won the opportunity to pick the name. After having three daughters, a wife, two female guinea pigs, and now two female dogs, and in great need of something masculine in the house, I named this female miniature red dachshund Charlie. Little did I know that Charlie would become my shadow and dedicated companion. Everywhere I went, Charlie followed. When I went outside to hit golf balls from my backyard, she would run circles around me until I hit the ball, then run about sixty to seventy yards, pick up the ball, and bring it back. Charlie would do this as long as I would stay out there. In fact, Marie took Charlie to the vet once, and he commented he had never seen a dachshund with such large hip muscles! Charlie was a stud!

Before I was sick, Charlie would sleep with me and sit next to me while watching television. When I was sick, Charlie would sit by the door, waiting for me to come home, and could not understand where I was. When I was sick and at home, Charlie would sit in my lap. I later learned that dogs could smell the odor in my stomach given off by the cancer. Charlie got to visit me in the hospital during one of my monthlong stays. It was hard to tell who was happier that day. It was a great spirit lifter for me. Unfortunately, we lost both dogs later in my illness. Marie had to deal with all this alone, and I know it was hard on her. It seemed as if death and illness were all around us.

One morning in early May, Lynn, my nurse, and I were watching *Law & Order*. We had just finished my morning physical therapy, and I was in my usual weird stupor—tired after PT and just staring at the TV. It was about eight thirty in the morning when suddenly the door from the garage opened and Marie walked in from work. I could tell something was wrong. She sat down next to me, grabbed my hand, and told me my eighty-six-year-old dad had committed suicide by sticking a shotgun in his mouth and pulling the trigger. I was in disbelief and just felt such despair and confusion. Here I was, fighting for my life, and my dad had ended his life. What? Was this a bad dream—the worst bad dream ever—that was actually true? I had no understanding. I had experienced several near-death experiences fighting cancer with all I had, and Dad had done this? How should I respond? Should I cry? Feel angry? I did both of those things, but what the hell? My younger brother Kent found my dad in the basement. How horrifying for Kent. I considered how tragic it was that Dad's youngest little baby found him that way, and I wondered how Kent would handle this picture for the rest of his life. I needed my dad's support, but he did this.

I often felt negative feelings about people that committed suicide. That was wrong; I should not have judged people in this way. We can't understand the demons they struggle with. My brothers Barry and Kent, who lived close to Dad in

Columbus, Ohio, were wonderful in helping him. But none of us understood the depths of Dad's depression.

My friend Bryan Mills explained to me that there are many doctors that feel suicide is like a heart attack. The brain cannot handle any more, so somehow the cure is to take your life. It is a misunderstood mental health issue. My mom had passed away five years earlier, and my dad had been very dependent on her for most everything. I am sure he was lonely and probably depressed, but he was mostly healthy physically. We never knew how troubled he was. While we talked to him when we could, we were so busy with my recovery that we couldn't take on much more at the time. I wish he could have reached out. But that takes courage and faith. I regret that my health kept me from helping him, but I was fighting for my life.

I never did really grieve Dad's death until many months later, when I watched the most recent remake of *A Star is Born* and witnessed the depression of Bradley Cooper's character and his suicide. I cried uncontrollably for several minutes. It just hit me, and suddenly it was all very real to me. So dark, so sad, so nauseating. I decided after my breakdown, though, that I could not let this hinder my recovery. I am a survivor, and this was one more challenge for me to overcome. With faith in God, I would do just that.

The day you receive your transplant is called "day zero" in the medical world. Each day after is a "+" day. After being discharged on day +18, my next goal was to make it to day +100 posttransplant with good test results. These tests give the doctors a good indication of how well the transplant is working. The Who's Who test was done frequently to determine whether my donor's stem cells continued to do their job and kept my old cells from trying to return. My many daily medications made sure my body didn't reject the new stem cells and helped keep me safe from infections and viruses that could have been devastating. I honestly don't remember much of this period. In writing this book, Marie has asked me to include more details about what I was going through, but I am so tired of explaining the suffering that I feel as if I have worn out my welcome. The antirejection medications made me very loopy! I couldn't concentrate on reading anything or even follow a television program. But Marie, Lynn, and the kids took me to many doctor appointments and made me do my physical therapy. No one gave up on me even when I could barely write my own name. Marie gave me homework every day with simple math questions and had me practice writing. I was not a willing participant in these activities! It was so hard to concentrate, and the neuropathy in my fingers made writing very difficult.

I reached my day +100 milestone on Easter weekend. We celebrated this with a big family dinner. I was still struggling a little with my concentration and energy levels. But I was improving. We continued to gauge my progress weekly. Trying to see daily progress was too frustrating for everyone. Our middle daughter, Kelleigh, gave me a card on Easter Sunday congratulating me on reaching my day +100 milestone. It also said that exactly five hundred days prior, I had first been diagnosed with lymphoma. And it added that in about two hundred days, we would be meeting our third grandchild! Kelleigh and Drew had not told anyone. We were all staring and a little quiet until we realized what the note was telling us! Kelleigh was pregnant with her first child! The next few minutes were chaotic, with crying, laughing, hugging, and looks of wonder. Tears of joy ran down my face as Kelleigh commented that I had another reason to fight for my life. Yes, indeed, I sure did!

The next goal was to make it to day +180, which would be the Fourth of July. Independence Day—how appropriate! In mid-May, I was finally able to stay by myself while Marie worked. I continued to exercise, took lots of meds, and tried to eat enough to regain some of my lost weight. I couldn't stand for any length of time, still needing to be driven to doctor appointments, and just completing simple daily tasks was tiring.

It felt odd to be in a world where I would most likely not need chemo again. Chemo had been a part of my life for over a year. I wondered how my body would respond to everything it had gone through during the last year and a half. I hoped the cancer wouldn't return and the transplant would continue to be a success. Remember: the stem cell doctors could not give us any idea how I would recover, or not recover, from the transplant. My quality of life was still in question. I was making progress with my physical and occupational therapy, but it was slow and painful. I wasn't sure whether I would ever be able to work again. Would I be able to support myself and Marie? I was fifty-seven years old—not old enough to retire. But was I too old to start a new career? This was scary, but our faith gave us hope. In the past, I took a lot of my life for granted. Would anyone find my value as an employee if I were not as strong or able as I had been prior to cancer? I was still in the land of the unknown. Yes, I was alive, and I was grateful. But did I have value to an employer or as a husband, father, or friend? Would I ever be the whole me again? I wanted to be known not as a survivor but as a thriver. I didn't know whether I would ever be me again. In my gut, I felt I was going to live. But now what?

The Fourth of July arrived, and I was continuing to improve. We had made it to day +180! I was working hard doing everything I could to make progress: exercising, eating well, managing the daily pain, going to doctor appointments, and praying the transplant would not be rejected. The list of long-term issues of a stem cell transplant is a long one. Just about every system in one's body can be damaged by it. Reading the list is scary! Marie was constantly watching for any sign that I was showing signs of rejection or long-term graft-versus-host disease symptoms. Heart, lung, skin, muscles, bones, joints, skin, eyes, ears, gastrointestinal organs, liver, kidney, bladder, nerves—any system or organ can be affected by a stem cell transplant.

As the summer of 2017 continued, I had a lot of bone pain, neuropathy, headaches, and achiness. These things had improved some but still were a strain on my body. My stamina was low. I tried acupuncture, which was a temporary help. Have you ever had one hundred needles in your head or twenty-five needles in your feet? It was like a different pain that helped a current pain. I began seeing a pain specialist also, which helped significantly. After we discussed all of my symptoms, my current pain management plan, and what my goals were, she prescribed the lowest possible dose of methadone. I know, I know, it's what is used to help opioid addictions. However, the methadone helped a lot more than hydrocodone. Depending on my pain level, I took one or the other. This really took the edge off of the pain and helped me move forward with more activity. I wish I had done this sooner, as it helped tremendously. As soon as the pain got better, I was taken off the methadone.

I was finally able to start driving in August. I was able to follow my buddies at the golf course and enjoy being outside again. I then was able to hit a few shots and started playing a hole or two in September. What a treat. By now it had been two years since I had played golf. The course I played had a lot of tees that were elevated, making it a chore to walk to the tee with my poor balance. I fell down a few times, but my friends helped me up, and after a good laugh we would just keep playing. These friendships were also important to my continued recovery; these were the guys that showed up at the hospital many times to just sit with me. In the beginning, I would only keep track of the pars I made, which sometimes were none! My doctors all agreed that golf turned out to be great physical and mental therapy for me. I kept playing golf and made six pars in a round before the season ended. For a guy who has been a scratch golfer, six pars isn't good at all. But considering what my body had been subjected to in the last two years, I was thrilled with those pars. When it got cold, I would go for walks at Wolf Run Golf Club, searching for lost golf balls. It was a thrill getting back to nature after spending so much time inside hospitals and my house. There's nothing like the crisp smell of fall and the beauty of the outdoors.

Now that I was able to walk and stand for longer periods of time, I was able to start lifting weights to build my strength. I would use ten-pound dumbbells and flexible bands, and I did exercises using the walls or steps of our house. I found it interesting how my mind worked during rehab. I found myself reflecting on two-a-day football practices during high school and how hard those practices were. It made me feel confident I could get through rehab too. Dr. Dugan advised me to push myself to maximum pain each day, and then rinse and repeat. Doing this helped strengthen me mentally and physically though it was exhausting. I would often sleep ten to twelve hours per night *and* take an hour nap during the day. Marie could tell by looking at me or the sound of my voice when I needed those extra hours of sleep. And she was always right.

Since I was finally able to drive again—it having been almost a year since I had driven—I was able to go to outpatient physical therapy. My therapists were very patient and helpful with my development. I then graduated to going to the rehab center of our local hospital, which had every machine possible, plus free weights and a walking track. I followed my doctor's advice and worked out until I maximized the pain and then repeated the process the next day. When I started, I could not do even one push-up. I teased the kids in early November that I would be up to one hundred push-ups by Christmas!

They didn't believe me—which was smart, as I only made it to sixteen. By February of 2018, I had made it to twenty. I may never make it to one hundred, but I will never stop trying.

In early November, I registered to participate in the tenth annual Michael Treinen Foundation 5K Turkey Trot on Thanksgiving Day to help raise money for the Indiana region of the Leukemia & Lymphoma Society. Our friends Tom and Kelly Treinen lost their son Michael to AML when he was nineteen years old. I had the privilege of coaching Michael in soccer when he was five and he and Kelleigh played on the same team. Michael was a joy to be with, and I will never forget his beautiful smile. I told Marie I wanted to participate in the 5K even though I wasn't sure I would be able to finish. It was a chilly day, and the sun came out to warm us up. Caroline was by my side every step of the way. I came in dead last, but it was the biggest athletic accomplishment of my life. Marie was waiting at the finish line with tears running down her cheeks. It was a magical day.

On January 5, 2018, we reached my one-year anniversary of my stem cell transplant. Reaching this goal has allowed me to move forward with high optimism. My body still has a long way to go and most likely will never be the same. I continue to have side effects, and getting older is working against me as well. We asked the doctors, "When will I be cured?" But no one is ever cured of cancer. One doctor said one year past transplant—another said two years—gave me the best chance of no recurrence. Of course, no one knows. My pain specialist put it best when she said, "We call this the invisible finish line." A transplant is a race that never ends. It may appear to others that I am recovered or "over it," but I will deal with issues every day for the rest of my life. That doesn't mean my life will be horrible; it just means that recovery from a transplant never ends.

In late spring, Marie decided it was time to sell our house.

I thought *What*? We had lived in this house for over twenty years. It was always my dream to live on a golf course, and we lived next to the green of the third hole of our golf course. This was our second home on this golf course. I had a professional putting green upstairs in my house. Did I mention I love to play golf! But like most wives, Marie was right. The kids were out of the house, there were too many stairs, and it was very difficult for Marie to keep up such a large house. Marie reached out to longtime good friend Linda Petit Carey, who was also a realtor. Linda is one of my favorite people in the world. She possesses the most natural charm and sense of humor of any person I have ever met, and she is also a great golfer. Marie and Linda worked together to build our new home.

Marie

January 2018

AT TODD'S ONE-YEAR TRANSPLANT APPOINTMENT, THE TRANSPLANT coordinator came in and asked whether Todd would like to contact his donor. Todd immediately said, "Yes!" He completed some paperwork and was told someone would be in contact with him if his donor also agreed to the contact. We were hopeful the donor would agree.

On January 12, Todd received an email from the hospital that gave him his donor's name and contact information. Todd called me over to see the email. It was a moment when time stopped for a couple minutes. We were looking at the name of the person who had selflessly given Todd something we could not get anywhere else that saved his life. Todd's donor was Glenn Thornton, and he lived in Boise, Idaho. Todd emailed Glenn, and they set up a phone call for the next morning. Todd was excited to speak with this generous man. He called him his blood brother. And then he asked me, "How do you thank someone for saving your life?"

Our phone call with Glenn was not what I thought it would be. Todd put Glenn on speaker so I could participate. I was appreciative of that. I said to Glenn, "Thank you for saving my husband's life." And you know what Glenn said? "No, he saved my life." Todd and I looked at each other in disbelief. How could Glenn say that?

Glenn continued telling us that when he received the call from DKMS asking him to be a donor, he "finally saw a tiny birthday candle a mile away at the end of a tunnel," referring to his tunnel of grief from losing little Errol just six months prior. He told us donating "gave [him] a reason to be alive again." Glenn had been swabbed several years prior at the Treefort Music Fest, which is held in Boise each spring. We are so glad something made him stop at that booth!

Glenn gave us some insight into the process of donating. He was flown to Seattle twice: the first time to be medically cleared to donate, the second time to make the donation. And in between he had to take some medication and receive some injections to boost his cell counts. He made it sound so simple. I was so grateful he had been willing to do all of that.

We both were also aware from the redacted letter Todd had received from Glenn that he had lost his two-and-a-half-year-old son. But we didn't know any other information about it. Through his tears, Glenn told us about the tragedy of losing Errol and how he had been trying to do the right thing by straightening out his life of addiction by going to rehab. It was so shocking hearing Glenn's story. What we had been through was nothing compared to Glenn and Season's loss of Errol. We were in awe that Glenn and Season were so willing to help someone else even as they felt such numbing pain.

Todd and Glenn talked a lot about how humans need to have each other's backs to get through life and that being kind is paramount. The connections of humanity are what get us through tragedy, pain, disappointment—all the crappy parts of life.

Our call ended with them telling each other they would stay friends forever. I don't think that will ever be a problem.

Glenn

January 2018

I RECEIVED AN EMAIL FROM DKMS, THE DONOR REGISTRY. THEY said my recipient was alive and doing well. He wanted to contact me. His name was Todd Irwin, and he lived in Noblesville, Indiana. I could not contain my excitement! I had so much that I want to tell him. I hoped he wouldn't think I was nuts when I explained all the crazy miraculous things that had happened inside my soul because I got to help him. We planned to talk on the phone that weekend. My heart was so full of love for that guy and his family, and we hadn't even spoken yet. I hoped he would believe me when I told him how much he helped me through my grief. I just wanted him to realize that his suffering wasn't meaningless. Fingers crossed.

Todd and Marie and I talked on the phone for the first time on January 13, 2018. We talked for about an hour. This day changed my life forever. We shared our stories of love, loss, perseverance, redemption, and faith. It was clear to us immediately that this story was bigger than the two of us. An opportunity had been placed in front of us. I felt something on the phone with Todd and Marie that I had never felt before. I felt I was still alive for a reason.

Losing Errol took everything from Season and me. We could never escape the feeling of being cheated. We are good people who care about others and want to leave a positive impact on the world. When Errol passed, I struggled for a long time with these feelings that I was getting what I deserved and that his death was my fault. He wouldn't have been at my parents' house if I hadn't needed to go to treatment. Mostly I

124

was angry that something like this could happen to Season. Season did everything right and did it effortlessly. I'll say it again: Season and Errol saved my life.

I've been going to a trauma therapist since Errol's death. I know that I'll never be able to reconcile his loss completely. I've learned to deal with my feelings and emotions in healthy ways. I've learned to run toward them, not away from them. I'm addicted to fishing now! It could be worse—it *has* been worse! I've also been getting help from another amazing therapist. I call her my spiritual therapist. She's helped me reconnect with that spirit that is inside us. She is amazing!

Truthfully, I was terrified when Todd asked me to contribute to his book. I wondered whether these people would accept me for all that I am and all of my experiences and imperfections that had led me to this point. They knew me only as some guy that donated stem cells, not a hopeless, dying addict. Well, they did accept all of me, and if you know Todd and Marie, then you are not surprised by this in the least. They're old souls, those two. The love that they have for each other is akin to the love that Season and I have—true love. The bond that Todd and Marie have because of what they've been through is the same bond that Season and I have after losing Errol. It's unbreakable and eternal.

Todd

January 2018–March 2018

I DIDN'T KNOW HOW AWKWARD THE CALL MIGHT BE. I KNEW NOTHING about Glenn or his life. But I was excited to talk to him and thank him for donating his stem cells to me. We set up the call for a Saturday afternoon. As soon as Glenn answered, we thanked him for saving my life. And you know what Glenn's response was? "No, you saved my life!" We were puzzled to say the least. I thought, *He has this backward!* Glenn told us all about sweet Errol. Learning about Glenn's history of addiction and their traumatic loss of Errol brought us to tears. Our phone call was overwhelming, and we remained stunned while trying to process this incredible gift. I knew he was a giving man before the call, but after our conversation I knew that description was not even close to what Glenn truly is. He is so courageous, humble, and loving. Glenn's stem cells run through my body, healing me every day. What more can a person ask for? Glenn overcame incredible adversity and graciously and literally saved my life. Without Glenn's compassion for helping me, I would not be here today. His son's life and spirit saved my life and spirit. I felt I needed to meet Glenn, Season, and their four-month-old son, Elliot, and thank them in person soon.

Glenn and I talked several more times in the next month, and we decided it was really important that we meet each other in person. So we need more drama, right? How about this: several years ago, Glenn was swabbed for the DKMS stem cell registry while he was working the Treefort Music Fest in Boise. Glenn handled the audio for the many bands at the festival. Over four hundred bands play over several days of the festival. For some reason, he took the time during one of his busy days to get swabbed. It takes only a few minutes, and something compelled him to stop and get swabbed. And, boy, are we glad he did! In 2015, stem cell and bone marrow donor registries reached over 25 million registrants—that's the year I got sick. And out of those 25 million selfless people, Glenn's stem cells were the best match to me. Even my own brothers weren't as close a match as Glenn. DKMS was started in 1991 by a man in Germany. He lost his wife to leukemia because at the time there were so few donors that could be searched for a match. He was another person that took a negative and turned it into a positive. Think about how amazing that is. And even more astounding is that Glenn immediately said yes when he was asked to donate.

We decided to meet in March 2018, with DKMS sponsorship, where the stem cell story really began—at the Treefort Music Fest in Boise. We wanted to raise awareness for stem cell donations. So it was decided that we would meet in person for the first time on stage in front of the festival crowd of people.

As we prepared for our trip to Boise, I had so many thoughts. Who was this guy that saved my life? I didn't care what he looked like; I just wanted to thank him. There's no way to prepare for the feeling you have when someone has saved your life. What he went through with Errol that led him to decide to donate his stem cells was so heart-wrenching. Glenn was so selfless in helping me while dealing with his own challenges. What we had been through was nothing like what he and Season were going through.

Our trip to Boise was overwhelming, but it was overwhelming in a great way. I was not yet at full strength, and we were a little concerned about how I would handle the travel and excitement. We decided it would be a good idea for our youngest, Caroline, to go with us to help and meet Glenn and Season with us. The DKMS CEO at the time, Carina Ortel, came to Boise from New York to facilitate our introduction. Marie, Caroline, and I were kept hidden in a hospitality tent, along with Carina, until the big moment. Carina met Glenn on stage to tell the crowd about the enormous need for donors and how easy it is to donate. Glenn then had the courage to tell his emotional story of addiction and the devastating loss of Errol. Season was in the crowd with infant son, Elliott. We stood at the edge of the stage steps, listening with tears in our eyes, our hearts about to jump out of our chests, and an enormous feeling of gratitude.

Carina introduced me, and I gingerly walked up the stage steps to Glenn's open arms. We hugged on stage, crying for what seemed like five minutes. The hug was pure joy. I felt very alive in that moment. And the folks of Boise cried right along with us. Within a few minutes, we all went from sadness to celebrating life. It was almost too much to handle! I pulled myself together to tell the crowd a little more about my hero, Glenn, and how his generosity impacted our entire family. I tried to make sure that everyone saw the importance of human kindness and the need to help each other. I also told them I felt that my stem cell transplant was the best oil change of my life! After more hugs offstage, we got to meet Season and Elliott. We then headed over to the DKMS tent. We watched many people stop by to sign up and get swabbed. That was really cool to watch. A couple of Boise news stations covered our meeting, so Glenn and I were interviewed, and that allowed us to spread the word even further. Our families were able to spend some time getting to know each other afterward. We enjoyed every minute we had with Glenn, Season, and Elliott. And I finally felt able to move forward to my next stage of life: the survivor stage.

I Lived Because I Was Loved

Here is the link to one of the interviews with Glenn and me after we met each other: https://www.ktvb.com/article/news/local/men-connected-through-life-saving-donation-meet-at-treefort/277-532037791.

129

Todd

January 2019

EACH YEAR PAST TRANSPLANT IS ANOTHER YEAR CLOSER TO BEING less likely the cancer will return. My doctors can't definitively say when, if ever, I will be 100 percent cured. "Cured" is not a word they like to use. I am constantly trying to improve my body with swimming, yoga, walking, lifting weights, and playing golf. I enjoy the challenge of mixing up activities. I also work on my mind to set the pace of my life and priorities. My faith in God has given me a sense of contentment. I thank God for the miracles he has provided. God deserves so much glory.

After all these physical challenges, I had to pursue a new job. Once I received medical clearance, I spent many months looking for a new position. It was mentally challenging, tough on my ego, and humbling. I hope none of you will ever have to experience this challenge if you have faced a life-threatening condition. God taught me a lot as I faced the unexpected need to truly understand forgiveness. I am now thoroughly enjoying a career in sales consulting. For this I am extremely grateful.

Marie

January–July 2019

OUR STORY COULD HAVE EASILY BEEN MUCH DIFFERENT. IT COULD have ended in the first few pages of this book. The lymphoma could easily have taken Todd's life. That fact is not lost on us. During editing, I asked Todd many questions about how he felt at certain times. Sometimes he just honestly couldn't remember, owing to the side effects of medications he had to take and the pain he endured. But other times, after some thought and maybe some coaxing from me, he came forth with feelings I never knew he had and wrote them down. I think of the many lonely hours he had in the hospital—especially after the transplant. He didn't leave that hospital room even once for nineteen days. It was not a large room! It was January in Indiana, and it was bleak and gray and cold. Looking out the window didn't do much to help anyone's mood. Todd's personality is vibrant; he never meets a stranger. He also loves to be on the go all the time. Being confined the way he was had to be very difficult for him. I am so proud of Todd for finding the strength to fight day after day after day for two and a half years. I try to tell him often how thankful I am that he fought to stay with us.

We have officially celebrated Todd's two-year anniversary of his stem cell transplant that was done on January 5, 2017. Has it gone fast? Nope. Has it been hard? Yep. Was it worth it? Absolutely. That may be an obvious answer, but the transplant doctors were honest with us from our very first meeting, telling us that stem cell transplant recovery is hard, that it may not work (with a 40 percent chance of it working for Todd), and that there were no guarantees of his end condition. Our family accepted those risks because we wanted no regrets.

And remember the Ohio State needlepoint belt I began making during the week of Todd's transplant? It took a while, but I finished it, and he wears it often! It's a good reminder that we kept a positive outlook in the worst of times during his transplant recovery.

So what is our reality? For Todd it means his body almost always hurts. His neuropathy will probably never go away. He still struggles with his stamina. His taste buds don't work very well. His head is still bald. The chemo has taken a toll on his teeth, eyes, and bones. He still takes numerous medications twice a day. He still experiences frustration at what these last three years have changed for him and our family.

Todd couldn't work for about two years. Then he spent six months finding a new job. It was a long six months. Our finances took a big hit, but we were blessed to have good insurance. I was able to continue working with the help of family and friends, and I watched our budget like a hawk. I learned that a lot of necessities were not necessities. While our financial life is different now, we have all we need. Most importantly, we have Todd.

As for me, I have struggled with giving up the caregiver role. I still jump up in bed every time he gets up in the middle of the night because I'm afraid he will fall or is feeling ill. I can instantly tell how he really feels just by hearing his voice. In church recently, Todd's hands started trembling. I thought he was having a seizure. But he was just being goofy while the choir sang an upbeat song! I recently let him start sorting his medications each week (but I secretly check to be sure they are correct)! I set out snacks for him to take with him when he has long days. I wish I could stop, but for close to three years I managed every aspect of his life. I've read that it can take a caregiver longer than the patient to move forward. I would say that is accurate in my case.

To this day, I struggle watching television shows and movies in which someone is diagnosed with cancer. And my gosh, there are so many of them! When I have forced myself to watch one, I can't help but think the people making them have never experienced cancer, because they sure sugarcoat it. What cancer really looks like is not pretty, and it is so hard on everyone involved. I guess that is just not what people want to watch. One series I watched recently, *From Scratch*, came a little closer to the realities of cancer, and while I sobbed several times through it, I also felt seen.

Every journey has life lessons that can't always be seen when you are in the thick of it. When we look back now, we see a lot of good things that happened along the way. Some are the miracles that Todd has written about. Some are complex, such as learning each family member's strengths. Some are simple, such as appreciating the day Todd really enjoyed a piece of dark chocolate again after chemo messed with his taste buds. And some make you realize that God's hand is in all the lessons. I feel certain that the AML diagnosis happened when it did so the transplant could completely heal Todd's blood. Even the doctors can't explain why the AML happened so quickly after remission of the lymphoma. God is great all the time.

There are so many positives we choose to focus on in our lives. We have three grandsons now, and they give us immense joy. Our family forever knows we will always have each other's backs, even when it means wiping each other's tushes! We all push ourselves a little harder to celebrate even the smallest accomplishments together. We enjoy silly group texts. The kids call out their dad when he tries to pull the cancer card on them. Our roots were deep when our nightmare began, but they grew deeper and wider and stronger than we ever knew possible. And we know without a doubt that we can do hard things. Good can come from tragedy. God is always there. But you have to open your eyes to find all these things.

One consequence of everything we went through was something we didn't even realize until many months after Todd began recovering. Our discussions about it caused us a little bit of a shock because it didn't even cross our minds until it was resolved. As Todd became weaker as the treatments continued, we lost our identity as a couple. We lost *us*. When Todd was diagnosed, we had just entered the "empty nest" stage of life. But our empty nest sure was different from anything we ever expected. Of course we probably spent more time together than we usually would, but it was a different type of togetherness than in past years. There were many months when even kissing was dangerous because his immune system was so compromised. There were no date nights. We couldn't even order takeout because of Todd's suppressed immune system. We didn't discuss our children or our finances, and we couldn't make any future plans—we weren't sure we had a future. Our conversations centered around how he felt, what he ate, and the next doctor appointment. And at one point in his stem cell recovery, we didn't even have those conversations because Todd's brain was so addled. It was up to me to take care of everything beyond his hospital room for our lives: our home, pets, cars, insurance, bills, financial decisions, medical paperwork, and so on. We received notice from the IRS that someone had tried to fraudulently file our income taxes early during his illness. I really needed that! There were many things I didn't want to burden him with, so I just took care of it. I wish we had figured out some way to connect as a couple instead of as patient and caregiver during that time. We now finally feel like a couple again, and we are starting to hope and dream! But it's sad to think that we lost those years.

The medical paperwork from Todd's two cancers and stem

cell transplant fills more than three plastic file bins to this day. It's hard to know where to even start with hospitals, insurance companies, disability, government agencies, and even go-between companies we were required to work with during Todd's treatment and recovery. And I still deal with many of these agencies on a weekly basis. Our medical insurance decided to stop covering him, which resulted in an enormous five-figure debt. A government agency had me fill out three forms for disability coverage that were all incorrect, and this resulted in delays of more than eleven months. I discovered an overpayment that I brought to a government agency's attention, and when I asked how to repay them, I was told to wait for a letter from them. That letter took over six months to arrive, and I promptly repaid them. Considering everything that can be done through technology—scanning, signing, emailing, completing forms—none of our government systems utilize these abilities. Everything is paper and is sent through USPS mail, which delays coverage and payments. I have completed hundreds of forms and sent copies of billings, invoices, and diagnoses. When I call with questions, I rarely speak to a live person; and if I do, I have to have Todd by my side to give them permission to speak to me concerning his coverage. And the wait times on calls are usually long.

I say all this to try to make sense of why our government makes health care so difficult, confusing, unclear, and baffling. I cried so many times on the phone after being told I was wrong yet again and it wasn't their problem. According to them, it was my responsibility to read, research, and understand each and every detail of the government agency policies. All the while, I was just trying to keep someone who needed 24-7 care alive while I worked full-time and slept an average of four hours a night. At one point when Todd could hear my frustration on another phone call, he said to me, "Maybe it would have been easier if I had just died." Talk about a kick in the gut! That is not what someone should feel while fighting for his or her life. There's a popular saying: "Being kind is free." Kindness is a form of love. I wonder when our government will start legislating with kindness.

We know we will never be able to adequately thank our medical teams, our extended family, our amazing friends, and our coworkers. The practice of medicine is miraculous, and the people who practice it every day are heroes, plain and simple. All of our families were so gracious and willing to help us in many ways. That includes our son-in-law's families as well. Our daughters and sons-in-law were just amazing. Our friends went above and beyond every day to be sure our needs were met. Our coworkers stepped up and did our jobs when needed. And our prayer warriors—I wish I had a count of how many prayers were said worldwide. "Thank you" isn't sufficient to each and every person who supported Todd and our family. Each of them was instrumental in saving Todd's life.

Our family feels unending gratitude to someone we never had the pleasure of meeting—sweet Errol. My heart aches knowing that Glenn and Season have suffered so much. But even as they suffered, they found the love and willingness to help when asked. I have a small stone with an angel on it that I touch each morning. I think of Errol as that angel and thank him for the gift he gave our family, and I ask him to take good care of his daddy and mommy and baby brother, Elliott. Errol's gift is felt every day by each of us. I pray that Glenn and Season feel it too.

PART 2

Thoughts from Family and Friends

We said in the beginning that we wanted you to hear how our family and friends felt throughout Todd's two cancer battles and his stem cell transplant. Journeys like ours affect so many people. The lives of our family and friends were disrupted too. Maybe their thoughts will help you help someone you love someday. Our daughters' thoughts follow. Other friends' and family members' comments will follow their thoughts.

Katie Irwin Bransteter

Todd and Marie's Oldest Daughter

December 2015

THE SUMMER BEFORE MY DAD GOT SICK, I WAS COMMUTING HOME from the university where I teach. I had this random thought come into my mind and heart: "Your dad is going to die young." I remember the exact road I was on, but I brushed it off. I tend to be a big worrier, and I was trying to get better at putting things in perspective. I would learn later this was about the time Dad was starting to experience discomfort in his stomach on the golf course.

Fast-forward to Dad's first hospital stay, which resulted in exploratory surgery. I visited him in the hospital the night before his surgery, and for some reason I felt compelled to visit him early on the morning of his surgery before I went to teach. I also felt someone needed to be with Mom during the surgery for support, and I asked my sister, Kelleigh, if she could be there. As I was wrapping up the semester with my students, I could see that Kelleigh had called, but I couldn't answer. I texted her to give me an update, and she texted me back that I should call. I was walking to my car when Kelleigh told me over the phone. I almost threw up, literally. It was a feeling like none I'd ever had before.

I drove an hour directly to the hospital. I met my sister and Mom in the ICU family waiting room, and I will never forget the image of my sleeping dad being rolled into the ICU wing. All I could think about was how vulnerable he looked, and he didn't even know it. I'd never seen either of my parents in this way before, and I wasn't expecting to see them at their worst until we were much older. Little did I know that would be a whole lot of what life would be like for the next couple of years. It was amazing how quickly the day-to-day tasks that we humans do and spend so much of our time on just seemed so trivial and meaningless compared to the survival of my dad. I've since learned that the saying "Don't sweat the small stuff" is entirely right. The small daily things that humans tend to worry ourselves silly over really won't mean much at the end of our lives.

The moment following my dad's comprehension of his cancer was ironically a very humorous moment, which seems fitting for my dad. After my mom told him it was cancer, he immediately said, "Well, I've got to get to Shelbyville in a few days. I have an appointment with a customer." And we just looked at each other like, "Who's going to tell him this is not going to happen?" This has since become a family joke because it shows how difficult it is to understand the magnitude of a cancer diagnosis and the way in which the lives of those affected are completely and forever changed from all they've ever known.

And so the whirlwind began. Kelleigh, Mom, Dad, and I went to my dad's first oncology appointment and chemo teach so we could learn about the regimen of his treatment. When we got there, they told us that some things had changed and that we needed to wait while they reviewed some test results. That appointment was one of our most memorable. As the doctor told us the worst news about Dad's aggressive, rare type of lymphoma and laid it all out on the table for us, I saw real fear in my dad's eyes, but I gained a great sense of trust in Dr. Bhatia. He was running tests multiple times and consulting with doctors at MD Anderson Cancer Center in Texas, and time was of the essence. I remember sitting in the car with Kelleigh after the appointment. We were emotionally exhausted and were preparing ourselves to call our husbands and our youngest sister, Caroline, who lives in Chicago, to share the news. We were so thankful that Caroline's good friend Nikki worked with her so Caroline could have someone to go to in the middle of the workday as she received this frightening new information.

I remember going home that night and sitting on the floor of my family room with my husband. We just sat quietly. All I could say was "Why?" repeatedly. I felt trapped. I felt we had no way out. There wasn't anything I could personally do to make this cancer go away and bring my dad back to normal. As a teacher, I love leading others to success. I had to start praying because I felt it was the only thing I could control that may have an impact. I had to repeatedly tell myself, "Faith over fear," as my best friend, Amy, had shared with me as she heard updates. That became my mantra each time I found myself anxious and worried. I have always struggled with controlling my emotions, which is something my dad always had to help me with as I grew up.

To add to the drama, I had to reencounter a health issue of my own. Since high school, I have lived with Crohn's disease. It's not a fun chronic illness to discuss because it's an irritable bowel disease, and you don't necessarily look sick if you have it, so it's hard to explain. Since the day I saw my dad being rolled into ICU, I was constantly running to the bathroom on a never-ending basis. When I get emotional, I get flare-ups. When Dad unexpectedly started chemo treatments sooner than planned, my visits to the bathroom increased so much I ended up in the hospital. As I was lying in the hospital, my dad was in a hospital bed a few floors above me, with my mom at his side; my sister Caroline was at my house, lying in my youngest son's crib, trying to get him to sleep as my oldest son, Luke, slept just across the hall. My parents had no idea I was two floors below them, and they didn't need to know. It was all hands on deck, and I thank my parents for raising my sisters and me to be able to support each other through it all.

February 2016

My dad and I both were on a journey to achieve remission—
Crohn's for me and lymphoma for him. He sure did get the
short end of the stick. My sisters and our husbands were so
thankful to have flexible jobs in which we could rotate days
to take care of Dad as he went through each round of chemo.
Mom needed to work for insurance and financial reasons,
not to mention some relief from constant caretaking. The
one thing I can immediately say about chemo is it completely
sucks. It saved my dad's life, but the side effects are brutal.
The chemo regimen was one of the most intense one can
be given. On any given day, the following could happen: he
would pass out, pee his pants, need help walking, and become
very confused. He also demanded pain medication constantly
(including after we had just given it to him) because it was
not helping or he didn't remember taking it. We had to force
him to eat, to get out of bed, help him get dressed, help him
bathe—the list goes on. I remember that my dad's sickness
would creep up on me while I was doing simple things like
shopping at Target. I would see couples my parents' age
walking around, and all I could think about was how amazing
it would be if my parents could go out in public together,
because it would mean my dad was not so sick. My sisters
and I had to pay attention to holidays that would occur while
Dad was sick, such as Valentine's Day, to be sure we could
get something for Mom from Dad, even if he wasn't coherent
enough to make these decisions. I suppose that's when having
three daughters comes in handy! One thing that raised my
dad's (and mom's) spirits, no matter what, was having their
grandsons visit him as often as possible in the hospital or at
home. It didn't matter whether they just lay with him so Dad
could touch them or whether he was lying in bed with his
eyes shut in pain and was able to hear their little voices in the

background as they played. In fact, Dad often told us that hearing any familiar voice was comforting to his pain.

The family and friends who came to take care of Dad have no idea what kind of relief they provided for us. While I would do it all over again, there were days when it was dreadful seeing my dad in such pain, and then there was the guilt of knowing he had no option to "take a day off." In the meantime, my Crohn's disease was doing okay—not great, but I was getting by. Eventually I landed in the hospital again and had no choice but to step up my medications. Now, in 2018, my doctor and I are still making some tweaks as I listen to my body and find better ways to handle my stress. The doctors who have taken care of my dad are tireless, good listeners, and badasses.

February 2017

If we thought the lymphoma and leukemia treatments were rough, we had no clue what was to come following the stem cell transplant. Much of the time, my dad was incoherent as a result of what we now know were medication side effects. He couldn't process things, speak in a way that made sense, or even write. We feared he would be like this forever. We called his oncologist to get a second opinion, and—bless him—Dr. Bhatia came to the house to "lay eyes on him." He reaffirmed that this was more likely due to the cocktail of medications he was on and that he would go back to being himself as he gradually weaned off these drugs. It's astonishing how a drug can impact a person's daily functioning while also saving his or her life. Dad would ask me questions like "Are you getting married again tomorrow?" and "Why can't I have stripes like your husband?" He could barely stay awake, he would go in and out of sleep at all times—whether at home, in the car, or at doctor appointments and hospital visits. His sleep was not restful sleep. He would talk and make noises and make all kinds of motions with his hands and arms. I remember that at a particular transplant clinic appointment, I was making him eat a little lunch. He'd fall asleep mid bite and then make motions as if he were conducting an orchestra or punching someone. It was *bizarre*. If we told him he was not making sense, we'd just frustrate him, so we just learned to go with it or ignore it. At this point, we sisters and our husbands needed a break from this. We were so thankful that Lynn, the private duty nurse, came into our lives. She was like Mom—very detail oriented with everything—and what a blessing it was to know Dad was in good hands, because unfortunately his caretakers' lives were still going full speed ahead.

January 2018

There are a lot of perfectionists in the Irwin family. We love a good plan. We love to prepare for all possible scenarios that might unfold within our plan. We love details, and we love when things go exactly as we planned. Dad's diagnoses and our journey was obviously not in our master plan of life, but they certainly were in God's master plan. None of us will ever be the same people we were before this part of our lives began. We all have a new normal. There will always be hard days ahead because of grief for Errol's life, grief for the healthy lives we took for granted, and the lurking fear anytime my dad is not feeling well. But we have a lot of new and closer relationships than we had before, as well as a trust and faith in God giving us what we need even if we don't think we need it.

Kelleigh Irwin Fagan

Todd and Marie's Middle Daughter

December 2015

I WAS THE LUCKY DAUGHTER SELECTED TO SIT WITH MOM DURING Dad's surgery. My wise older sister just didn't feel right about Mom sitting alone. Before the surgery, I honestly didn't think we were going to get terrible news. Oddly, cancer didn't even cross my mind. So when I watched Mom walk up to the desk in the waiting room at the hospital to take the phone call from the surgeon from the operating room and saw her face, my heart started racing. She walked back over to me and told me what they had found: a tumor—and it had metastasized, meaning it had spread. That was one of the scariest things to me, that it had spread. We didn't know where it had spread, but we knew it was bad. It's weird the things you remember in times like those when time stands still. I recall that just as we found out about Dad's cancer, stories of the shooting in San Bernardino, California, were breaking. We couldn't watch the TV to distract us from the news we had just received, because it was too devastating to watch. Looking back, I realize I was probably not the best support for Mom that day. I immediately got on the phone and started calling my sisters and husband. That was therapeutic for me. And once I delivered the news to them, I reverted to my academic side and started writing down questions for the surgeon once we had a chance to meet with him after surgery. When we did meet with him, he was so kind and patient and honest. But his honesty was unnerving. He didn't have all the answers we had hoped for, and we could tell he wasn't encouraged by how much the cancer

147

had metastasized. But he was empathic and had gotten Dad through the surgery well.

The rest of the family started arriving, and they moved Dad from postsurgery to the ICU. I remember sitting in the ICU family waiting room as they wheeled him past us. He was asleep from the anesthesia. One of his nurses saw the fear on our faces and gave us a pep talk, reassuring us that he would fight and be okay. That moment has always stuck out to me about that day. This was our first encounter with tireless nurses, physician's assistants, nurse practitioners, and doctors that we would come to appreciate and know and lean on. As we continued waiting for him to wake up, we used the time to call and tell the rest of our family and friends. Every phone call was hard, but it was comforting knowing we were expanding the group of people both feeling our pain and giving us hope and comfort. As you have seen, that group of people turned out to be more critical to Dad's fight than we ever imagined.

While Dr. Bhatia had already earned our trust, one of those moments when we appreciated why doctors go to medical school and why they make the big bucks occurred when the chemo first began. Dr. Bhatia had to make a call whether to stop the chemo or not when Dad's pain level became almost unbearable. We had started the chemo earlier than the oncologist wanted, as he wanted Dad to have more time to heal from surgery since the chemo could cause life-threatening damage to the colon. But the cancer was growing too quickly. It was like a cancer race. Dr. Bhatia's decision was spot on correct!

September 2016

I was there when the doctor told us about the second cancer diagnosis. Our reaction this time was different but in so many ways the same. It was the same because my dad's resolve to fight AML was no different from his resolve to fight the lymphoma. But it was different because it was scarier. The old adage "Ignorance is bliss" was never truer. This time we knew what chemo was like, how Dad would change, and the time and attention that it would require from all of us. It was also the first time I thought Dr. Bhatia was scared. He is like anyone at the top of his field; he likes to know why things happen, and having an answer is helpful even if that answer isn't what anyone wants. Not knowing why Dad got AML so quickly after lymphoma stumped him (and still does). It was scarier; Dad was in critical shape and going downhill quickly. We got the diagnosis late at night, after dinnertime. He and Mom were able to make phone calls to the rest of the family to tell them the terrible news. By the time I got to the hospital the next morning, he was lying flat on his back, silent except for a few groans. The room was dark, he was covered up by several blankets, and he just wanted someone next to him, holding his hand. He was in significant pain. The nurses were moving so quickly to get the chemo started, which gave him much relief within the first day. I don't think any of us realized at the time what critical condition he was in, but it was tough seeing him like that.

Caroline Irwin

Todd and Marie's Youngest Daughter

December 2016

I GAVE MY DAD SOME ADVICE TO ADD A DISCLAIMER ABOUT THE gross stuff he was going to be describing about his cancer journey, but he didn't listen, so I'll give you one instead. It's not pretty, but I think it's important for you to hear what it's really like to go through the effects of chemo. You see nausea and hair loss on television and movies, but the reality is worse and depends on the person. I always struggled when people would ask me the simple, polite question "How's your dad?" because my dad wasn't good. Did they want to know all the details? Should I respond with the high-level vague response I gave the last person? I had watched my hero become weak and unable to take care of his own body. Not knowing whether it would ever improve was too scary to even think through. Even though it is gross, I now know that when I choose to marry, I will be sure my spouse will wipe my ass, change my commode, and maybe even change my diaper someday.

July 2017

One of my favorite quotes, from Robert Brault, is "Enjoy the little things, for one day you may look back and realize they were the big things." I love my dad talking about little moments like enjoying the sun and, even if it's extremely tiring, hitting golf balls. Smelling the grass and just simply being alive after countless days in the hospital are so appreciated and relished. In the past, he would have been out there hitting balls because he was pissed after a bad round of golf. (And a bad round of golf for him was a round above 75!) It's a mentality I am trying to continue. I tend to be impatient and a doer, but if I don't slow down to appreciate the little things, I'll miss out on what's truly beautiful and important in this short earthly life.

Bryan Mills

Friend of Todd and Marie

MY WIFE, CATHIE, AND I HAVE BEEN FRIENDS WITH TODD AND Marie for more than twenty years. While they have three girls and we have four boys, our children and we became friends with them through school, sports, and golf. As our children grew up and started their own families, our get-togethers became less frequent, but we've remained friends and enjoyed the times when we've been able to catch up.

Personally, I have always referred to Todd as "the Golfer." I've never known anyone who played more golf—or thought about, talked about, or practiced the game more. He's safely the most golf-obsessed person I have ever met. Who watches professional golf tournaments to analyze the golf swings of professionals? Only the Golfer. In addition, the Golfer was a very successful salesman and fabulously devoted father and husband, and yet he somehow recorded more than a hundred golf rounds per year.

I don't recall how long it had been since we had seen Todd, but in November of 2015, Cathie shared that Todd had had surgery and was home recovering. We decided to visit (we've lived a half mile apart for twenty-five years) and catch up. We had no idea what we were walking into or the battle that would follow, but I've often wondered what would have occurred had God not nudged us to visit.

After a few minutes of catching up, I asked Todd, "What the heck is going on?" Todd and Marie shared that exploratory surgery had found cancer. We shared our shock and concerns and then asked when he was going to see an oncologist. Todd replied he was waiting for a call. I recall pausing for what seemed like an hour and then saying, "That's bullshit!" He just found out he had cancer, and someone was going to call him when they had time? I recall their daughter Caroline saying, "Thank you!" (FYI, I'm the CEO of a health care system in Central Indiana.) I shared that I didn't care where Todd received his care; however, if they wanted me to intervene, I would get an appointment arranged quickly. Marie advised that she had Todd's recent lab tests and she would send them to me.

I received the labs the following morning. I immediately emailed them to Dr. Sumeet Bhatia (a fabulous medical oncologist and an even better person), and within minutes Sumeet called and said, "Bryan, he needs to see me now." I called Marie, and she and Todd went to Community MD Anderson Cancer Center North and met with Dr. Bhatia.

A few weeks later, I was hosting our oncology team at a Colts/Texans football game. Dr. Bhatia (who is medical director for oncology) was also in attendance. We spoke for a few minutes about Todd. He was concerned about Todd's cancer and its aggressiveness but wanted to give him as much time as possible to recover from surgery prior to starting chemotherapy. On my way home from the game, my wife, Cathie, called and shared that Todd and Marie were en route to the emergency room at Community Hospital North. I told Cathie I would head there and be home later. Todd, Marie, their daughters, and their sons-in-law were in the room with Todd. It was evident that Todd was in great pain, and they were worried about him. Had I not been with Sumeet that afternoon, I'm not sure that I would have called him. (This is my second "God moment" in Todd's battle.) I stepped out of Todd's room and called Sumeet. He said he would be on his way immediately.

What I witnessed in that ER room is something that I won't forget. Sumeet assessed the situation, reviewed the chart, and began sharing his thoughts and options with Todd and family. Within seconds, Sumeet was peppered with questions from everyone. It was apparent that they were all scared and had been thinking about these questions for many days. Sumeet has a stellar reputation as an extremely good oncologist (and he is), but his ability to calmly address these questions, engage with family, and provide responses and education in terms that all understood was magical. He appeared to have all the time in the world. The decision was made. Todd would be admitted, and chemo couldn't wait. Game on ... and the team were all aware of the goal, its risks, and that they needed to focus their prayers on Todd being healed enough from surgery.

Todd was in Community Hospital North for many days and weeks. I'm not sure how many during 2016 and 2017, but it accumulated to many months. His condition was very serious, and while his attitude could have easily taken a negative turn, it didn't. I soon learned that I had never really known Todd. He wasn't just the Golfer; Todd was a spiritual soul who used this difficult time (opportunity) to fellowship with others. He walked the floors, embraced and built relationships with the nurses and support teams, and exhibited the strength and insight to use his diagnosis to help others. I had the pleasure of visiting Todd many times, and each time I walked away with *joy* from the words of hope, comfort, and inspiration that Todd shared. *Note:* Recently one of our sons was hospitalized at Community Hospital North. During one of my visits, I said hello to a nurse whose face looked familiar. She smiled and proudly said, "Bryan, I was Todd's nurse. I heard that he was meeting his donor last weekend." Yes, Todd, his battle, and his story are life-changing for all of us who have had the pleasure of experiencing this journey with the Irwins!

Mike Murray

Friend of Todd and Marie

IF YOU ARE BLESSED ENOUGH TO POSSESS FRIENDSHIPS THAT HAVE endured over forty-eight years, which is almost 80 percent of my life, you will relate to this. My first memories of Todd are of playing basketball together at the age of ten. We were actually pretty good players at the time. Todd was one grade ahead of me in school. We were roommates in college and double-dated with our now wives. Todd and I have enjoyed competing over the years in various things from grades in school to flag football and golf. Because Todd was a year ahead in school, he typically experienced things in life first: first job, first to marry, and first kids come to mind. He was never afraid to give advice (sometimes too much!) and guided me to my career when he came home from class one day and said, "You know you can be a double major if you take these four extra classes as electives in logistics." This added major of logistics ended up being my career. So you get the picture. Most people pursue careers in different cities after college, and my wife, Dayna, and I did just that. But through the many years in different states, we kept in touch a couple of times a year. Every time we saw the Irwins, it was as though we had never been apart and were double dating again. It was easy. Maybe that gives you a flavor of our friendship.

Fast-forward to Marie's phone call about Todd's diagnosis. During such times, you have no words, no advice; all you can do is ask questions and listen. Specifically, I was asking what to pray for to help the Irwin family. The desire to help was truly there. I had been with General Mills for thirty-four years.

The company had recently downsized, and I was available to help. To my amazement, I got a phone call from Marie; she asked whether I could come for a week and help with Todd. This was at a time when the chemo treatments were really starting to affect Todd. I jumped at the chance.

I had several "I know" moments. I know Todd had a sense of humor through the whole process. He could not stand up without fainting, his rear end was raw from "chemo butt," and he did not eat much, but throughout he still threw out one-liner jokes. I knew Marie cared so much about Todd that nothing would stop her from getting him better. My eyes are moist even now when I think of her deep love for Todd. Marie had a journal of daily activities, medications, questions for doctors and nurses, and many, many other things for me to use each day. I would picture Marie "kicking ass" when someone messed with Todd or made a mistake. Respect and admiration come to mind when I think about her tireless care of Todd while managing bills, working, and coordinating schedules. I know Todd and Marie have friends and family who are second to none.

When the pressure gets turned up on people, their true nature comes out. I could see the true nature of the Irwin family during this time. I know Todd is a fighter. Period. As I saw his ashen color during chemo treatments, he would joke with nurses and lift their days. It was so beneficial when Todd got intravenous liquids, including blood. He would go from gray to his normal color in thirty minutes. Todd experienced many things the normal person will never have to experience and fought the whole way. I am not sure I could be that strong. I know Todd's driving love for his family continued to increase daily. For a competitive guy like Todd, a goal is important when the situation does not seem to have much hope. I imagine that during the daily grind of small victories in therapy, it was hard for Todd to see the improvements over time. I hear those improvements when I talk to him on the phone today.

I know God loves Todd and Marie. I don't know how people could get through this type of event without Jesus. God works all things for good for those who love him. Todd and Marie may have asked, "Why me?" but I never heard it. This experience drew them closer as a couple and, most importantly, closer to their Father in heaven. For that I am grateful. I want all my friends to be with Dayna and me in heaven and experience heaven on earth today. Continue to pray, pray, pray. That journey has truly started for Todd. Finally, I am so glad Marie called us. I am so lucky to have been able to pray, to spend time with Todd and Marie, and to get to know his girls in a deeper way. They are so valued by us. Most of all, I am grateful to God!

Dayna Murray

Friend of Todd and Marie

I HAVE SO MANY QUESTIONS TO ASK GOD WHEN I GET TO HEAVEN. Mike, my husband, always tells me we won't have any questions when we get there. We will be so filled with joy to be in the presence of God, we won't care about the questions. Yes, yes, I know this is not the world God created for us. We sinned and messed up the Garden of Eden, and now illness is in the world. But cancer really sucks.

One thinks that one has all the time in the world to do things and to be with people one loves. "We'll go on vacation together ... someday." "We should stop by Todd and Marie's on the way to Ohio ... maybe next time." "Let's call Todd and Marie ... Oh, it will take longer than we have." "We really should make sure that Todd and Marie know Jesus. Maybe next time we visit, we will talk about it." What if there is no tomorrow? What if there is no next time?

Here was a new fear: what if cancer kills Todd and he does not know Jesus? Todd is fun. I want him in heaven with me! Cancer has a way of peeling back all the formalities and allowing you to speak directly into the lives of those you love. Cancer puts a time frame around eternity. It was time to start the conversation. We asked Todd about his faith. Todd said that he didn't know much about the Bible, so we bought and sent him a good study Bible.

The cure to cancer is with Jesus. The cure for everything is Jesus. He can either cure you on earth or cure you by taking you home to heaven. But if you don't know him, even if you are cured on earth, you are a dead man walking. Am I happy that Todd is on the path to health? Very! Am I happy that Todd is closer to God than he has ever been? Ecstatic! I know I will have eternity to spend with Todd. Really, nothing else matters.

Peter Griffen

Brother-in-Law of Todd and Marie

"I LOVE GOLF, BUT GOLF DOESN'T LOVE ME BACK." I UTTERED THOSE words after hitting my golf ball down and to the left into a magnolia swamp where few, if any, golf balls ever landed. My golf buddies Jim, Jeff, and Todd guffawed at my words. Todd, my brother-in-law and the best golfer I know, had invited me to go on a golf trip with a couple of his country club buddies. Todd and I had always played a few rounds every year on our family beach vacation, but this was the first time I was included in such a trip. Truth be told, I do love golf with a passion, but I do not possess the work ethic I have seen in Todd as he has worked on his game. I am a horrible golfer who is a legend in his own mind. Despite my ineptness, Todd always treated me with as much respect as any golfer he played with, no matter his or her skill level. I came to appreciate Todd's dedication to his golf craft and understood the reason he was so successful playing golf.

When it was announced that Todd had been diagnosed with Burkitt's lymphoma, I could see the same single mindset and work ethic that Todd displayed in pursuing being the best version of a golfer that he could be in his approach to his battle with cancer. He took every twist and turn with the same steady "I am going to beat this" attitude. In golf parlance, he was grinding, not giving an inch.

Marie was so strong during this time. She did the most loops as Todd's caddy. I was privileged to assist in a small way, doing a couple of loops myself with Todd. During that time, we spent many hours talking about numerous subjects, laughing, crying, and reminiscing about family vacations and events we had been part of for more than thirty years.

Every time I had to leave after these visits, Marie and Todd would both be effusive in thanking me for helping; in reality, it was I that received most of the blessings during those times. I saw a brave and unyielding spirit in Todd that I have tried to apply to my own challenges in life, and I learned that you can persevere through just about anything with an abundance of love around you.

Rocco Morando

Friend of Todd and Marie

TODD AND I GREW UP ON THE SAME STREET AND WENT TO COLLEGE together. In fact, Mike Murray, Jimmy Gulick, Todd, and I all grew up in the same neighborhood and have maintained a strong relationship throughout our lives. Jimmy was the biggest knucklehead—mostly for the good. When I heard that Todd was diagnosed with a rare cancer, I was very sad; I had never had a close friend with such a serious diagnosis. You see, I have spent my whole career with a pharmaceutical company that makes drugs for cancer, so I understand the treatment and prognosis of cancer.

Immediately, I wanted to talk to him. We spoke a few weeks after his surgery. I listened to his brave story and his conviction to beat cancer. I told him that I was praying for his recovery and that I loved him. My goal was to stay close to him and use my knowledge to help validate his treatment journey. And by now you know Todd's treatment was brutal. The drugs used to treat an aggressive cancer like Todd's are wicked. It's a good thing Todd is a big dude, because his strength and resilience allowed him to battle the side effects of these drugs. It was very rewarding to accompany Todd on a few of his doctor appointments when Jimmy and I came to take care of Todd for a few days. Being there (through care, support, and prayers) for a friend in tough times is true friendship. Not only do I believe my friendship helped Todd during his cancer journey, but it was also truly rewarding for me.

Linda Petit Carey

Friend of Todd and Marie

TODD AND MARIE ASKED WHETHER I WOULD LIKE TO CONTRIBUTE to their book from a friend's perspective. I deliberated over exactly what kind of contribution I could make, and I decided it might be best to talk about friendship itself—that elusive connection between people that cannot be defined by the length of time you've known someone or how often you see each other, but rather by that rare bond that keeps you joined by the heart and makes life a little softer, kinder, and richer. I first heard about Todd's initial diagnosis from a close mutual friend just shortly after Thanksgiving 2015. I, like everyone that heard the news, was shocked. I guess I was more shocked than I would have been about any other friend because it was Todd—big, burly, smart-assed, larger-than-life Todd. I was no different from most people who are friends with someone that has just been diagnosed with a life-threatening disease. My first thought was "What do I say? What can I do? I don't want to intrude."

First, let me flash back in time a bit. I first met Todd and Marie in the late 1980s. We were young married couples trying to maneuver through the "awkward" years of raising young children and trying to make new friends all at the same time. We soon formed a tight group of similar-aged couples, all from different walks of life, who were also raising young children. Our bond was created by our love of golf and our children and our need to raise a little hell now and then. I think the friends you make when you are a young married couple and you are all attempting to raise children and establish a career are like the ones you make when you are in grade school. You're all thrown into a new life situation that makes you unsure of yourself and insecure, but somehow you find great comfort in a group of friends who are navigating the same uncharted murky waters, and, like you, have no compass or even a damn map! You hang on to them tightly because they are your safety net. They are experiencing the same frustrations, fears, and joys, so you turn to each other for advice and comfort. This makes lifelong friends—friends that you never lose that connection with no matter where your lives take you.

It was because of that bond that it was easy for me to reach out to Todd and Marie, even though we really had not been in each other's day-to-day lives since our kids were in high school. And although I don't think I had talked to Todd in at least a year or maybe two, our conversation couldn't have been more natural, comfortable, or powerful. I knew immediately that I had a stake in this diagnosis too and that my role was to do all that I could to help these two dear friends and their family fight this horrible disease. It is hard to watch someone you care about go through such pain, fear, and heartbreak and feel so helpless. It is true that we can never know what it must be like to be thrown into that kind of life-and-death struggle unless we experience it ourselves. Unless that happens, we do not know what it is like to get up every day, day after day, and face what must seem like a herculean task, or to keep our faith and not give in to resentment and despair. But we, as friends to those going through such monumental struggles, are *not* helpless. We can be part of this great fight if we are willing to jump into the ring.

So my advice to anyone who has a friend battling a serious illness—or life crisis, for that matter—is to not be afraid to get your hands dirty and keep them dirty until it's time to wash up. And by that I mean don't hesitate to call, visit, write notes and cards, cater meals, clean the house, or run errands. Be consistent and persistent—maybe even obnoxious. Your friend will let you know if he or she has had enough of you! Better this than to be the kind of friend who swoops in with comforting words and empathy at the beginning of a life crisis journey but fades away when the illness drags on and they soon jump to the newest, latest, and greatest crisis. I consider myself lucky to have been a part of the "Todd Squad" for the past two years. The Irwins have shown me that true love and a deep faith in God (and some damn good doctors) can indeed get you through just about anything life decides to throw your way. I only hope that if I am faced with a life or health crisis, I can face it with the same strength and grace and resolve as Todd and Marie. They truly are an inspiration, and I am grateful to be able to call them my friends.

PART 3

Moving Forward

Todd and Glenn

Errol's Gift

SO OFTEN HUMANS WONDER ABOUT THE PURPOSE OF A SENSELESS tragedy or a frightening diagnosis. We have found many positives in our journeys. Two families that knew not one thing about each other have found great love and appreciation for each other. We know that Errol saved both of our lives. There is something greater than all of us safeguarding us. Some call it God; some call it spirit. People argue about what it is, but deep down we're all talking about the same thing. It's love. We all ask, "Why are we here?" Glenn and I know the answer now, and it's been in front of us since day one. It is a collective purpose in life to help each other through life and love each other. Keep fighting, keep believing, keep loving. Have faith in your purpose, and never give up! As Glenn said in our initial phone call, "It's not how you start; it's how you finish." This is Errol's gift. I truly lived because I was loved.

Todd and Glenn

Life Now

GLENN AND SEASON ARE HAPPILY MARRIED, ENJOYING BEING parents to their son Elliot. Glenn loves to fish and camp. He travels the world handling audio for a well-known comedian's live comedy shows.

I, Todd, am four years past transplant, and am currently cancer-free. I have a second birthday to celebrate each year now on my transplant date of January 5. I love spending time with Marie and our daughters, sons-in-law, three grandsons, and new granddaughter, Emily May. I have rebuilt my career as a sales consultant in the refractory industry. I constantly work on my body to rebuild my strength. I pray the world's people find a way to work together in love. God is missing in the lives of too many people and is overlooked as the answer to all of our problems. I am thankful to God for all the blessings received. I urge everyone to feel God's grace and joy in all they do. And please just love each other. Remember that I lived because I was loved.

One more thing: remember when I was preparing for my transplant and I was told my blood type would change to my donor's blood type? My journey from O negative to A positive is complete. Glenn lives in me; he is my lifeblood.

Acknowledgments

If we had kept a list of each person we needed to thank from day one, the list would fill many, many pages. We are so thankful to each and every person who touched our lives in any way throughout our journey.

We are grateful to every member of Todd's medical teams at Community Health Network, Community Hospital North, Community MD Anderson Cancer Center North, and St. Francis Hospital Blood and Marrow Transplantation. Every single employee from these medical facilities treated Todd with concern and respect, as well as with great knowledge. We are forever grateful to Dr. Sumeet Bhatia; Tricia Short-Yoder, NP; and Courtney Burratto, NP; from Community MD Anderson Cancer Center North for every sound decision, word of encouragement, and their dedication to saving Todd's life. Heartfelt thanks also to Dr. Michael Dugan, Dr. Luke Akard, Dr. John Edwards, and Dr. Anand Tandra at St. Francis for their expert care and concern throughout the stem cell transplant process.

Without the support and love from our families, friends, coworkers, and church family, we would not be where we are today. You know who you are, and we are so thankful for you.

Thank you to Todd's private nurse, Lynn Pont. Your friendship was as important as your nursing skills.

Thank you to our prayer warriors, some of whom we have never met, all over the world. You were so willing to pray boldly and ask for complete healing for Todd. Praise be to God!

Our contributors to this book include many of the people who were in the trenches with us. Thank you for your willingness to fight with us no matter what you had to do to

171

help. We know it wasn't always easy or pretty! So, thank you to Bryan Mills, Peter Griffen, Mike Murray, Dayna Murray, Rocco Morando, and Linda Carey.

Thank you to our children, Katie, Eric, Kelleigh, Drew, and Caroline. You showed up day after day with your own strength. Katie was nurturing, Eric was steady, Kelleigh asked all the nerve-racking questions, Drew sat through the worst appointments without complaint, and Caroline provided comic relief. Each of you did things for your dad no child should have to do for a parent, and you did all of it with grace, humor, and love.

The light our grandchildren, Lucas, Chase, Sam, and Emily, bring us every day is what we call "grand love." Our hearts are full when we are with you. You helped Pops recover in ways you may not remember, but we hope you will understand as you get older.

And Glenn—you saved Todd's life when you were hurting the most. Because you loved Errol so much, you wholeheartedly helped Todd. That is love.

With much love to all,
Todd and Marie Irwin
toddmarieirwin@gmail.com

Todd Squad Blog

When Todd became ill, our girls decided a blog was the best way to keep the people informed of Todd's progress. Being a private person, I, Marie, very reluctantly agreed. But it turned out to be comforting knowing that so many that read the blog were also our prayer warriors. Caroline, Kelleigh, Todd, and I each wrote entries. We tried to keep it uplifting, and a little witty at times, because that buoyed us too. We didn't voice our difficult experiences much until we wrote this book. If you are interested in reading the blog, here is the link: https://thetoddsquadblog.wordpress.com/.